Dear CIPP/US student,

This book contains three exams to help you succeed in passing the CIPP/US exam. The exams should help you identify the areas in which you need to improve your knowledge, and should train you to answer all questions within the allowed time.

The exams are followed by an answer key for a quick scoring of your exam. After, the questions are repeated with the correct answer highlighted and explained. This should provide some insight into how questions can be phrased, and the common mistakes to look for.

Take 2.5 hours per exam. You are allowed to return to (unanswered) questions, but only within 2.5 hours. During the exam you will be able to 'flag' questions, so you can return to them easily if you have time left.

If you scored 80% or more on all three exams in this book, you should be ready for the exam!

Sincerely,

Franklin Philips

Exam 1:

1. Which of the following is false regarding state legislative bodies in the U.S.?
A. All states have two legislative bodies
B. Not all states have multiple legislative bodies
C. A percentage of states have two legislative body
D. All except for one state have multiple legislative bodies

2. Which of the following entities creates administrative laws?
A. The senate
B. The house of representatives
C. The Federal Trade Commission
D. The judicial branch

3. Administrative law is different from case law. Where is administrative law documented?
A. The Federal Trade Commission guidelines
B. The Federal Communications Commission guidelines
C. The Code of Federal Regulations
D. An executive order

4. If, at some point, the U.S. Constitution gets amended, which requirement has been met?
A. The president has issued an executive order
B. Three-quarters of the states have ratified the amendment
C. Congress has voted, and the amendment received a majority vote
D. The president did not execute a veto

5. Judges in the judicial branch are appointed by the president. Which of the following do not serve until death, resignation, or impeachment?
A. Supreme court judges
B. Circuit court judges
C. District court judges
D. None of the answers are correct

6. Which of the following signs proposed bills into federal law?
A. The house of representatives
B. The executive branch
C. The senate
D. Congress

7. When a legal decision includes the term 'stare decisis', what is likely the case?
A. The decision is (partly) based on a previous legal decision
B. The legal decision is setting a precedent
C. It concerns a decision at the federal level only
D. It concerns a decision at the state level only

8. A court does not always have the authority to hear cases in a particular area of the law. In that case, which of the following is missing?
A. Preemption of the relevant state law
B. Subject matter jurisdiction
C. Preemption of the relevant federal law
D. A contract that covers the subject in question

9. Which of the following is least likely true regarding case law?
A. Case law is based on common principles found in previous court cases
B. Case law is used to resolve civil and criminal disputes
C. Applying case law is a form of stare decisis
D. Case law decisions are binding on subordinate courts

10. Contracts can be a source of privacy protection. Which of the following is least likely true regarding contracts?
A. A fine issued for speeding after signing for receipt is not a contract
B. If only one party offers something of value, it is not a contract
C. You cannot enter into a contract without intending to be bound by it
D. You can sell your house and agree on the terms verbally, but having the terms in writing takes precedence

11. Which court only has jurisdiction over specific U.S. states?
A. State court
B. Circuit court
C. U.S. supreme court
D. European Court of Justice

12. Preponderance of evidence is most relevant in which of the following situations?
A. The Federal Trade Commission entered into a consent decree with an organization to fix the organization's privacy issues
B. A person suing a company for damages because of the mishandling of personal information
C. A privacy dispute in which a privacy officer mediates
D. In case there is strict liability

13. Tracking cookies can track which website a user has visited. Which law does that most likely violate?
A. The General Data Protection Regulation
B. The Fair and Accurate Credit Transactions Act
C. The Controlling the Assault of Non-Solicited Pornography And Marketing Act
D. The Health Insurance Portability and Accountability Act

Use this case for the next three questions:
In recent years many new hotels opened in California. You always had the ambition of working in the hospitality industry, and with your newly acquired privacy certification, you are going to give it a shot. After searching through all the job vacancy websites, you select the ten most interesting vacancies and send in your application.

Several of the hotels invite you for an interview, and one hotel even asks you to send in a photo of yourself prior to a final invitation to the interview. You find sending a photograph a little intrusive, and also likely to hurt your chances, so you decline and, in an effort to be clever, you add the message 'I would not be a good privacy officer if I obliged to your request, as any data gathered from the photo is irrelevant for assessing my suitability for the vacant position'. Eventually, you are offered a position, and start work at your second-choice hotel, as the privacy officer.

During your first week you familiarize yourself with the hotel's practices concerning the collection and use of personal information. Guests generally book a room through one of the well-known booking websites. This process includes the booking website transferring guest information, such as name, date of birth, credit card number, and address. The personal information is stored on the hotel's server, which is accessible from all other locations of the hotel chain.

When a guest arrives, additional personal information is requested. This concerns a copy of a form of ID and the information concerning the other guests in the room. All guests receive a personal code for the Wi-Fi, which allows the hotel to keep track of all guests' internet activity. The hotel does this in order to pinpoint which guest is responsible in case any illegal activities take place, and the internet activity is stored for six months.

14. After the hotel has been accused of overly invasive privacy practices, the Federal Trade Commission and the organization agree on changes to be implemented. No fine is issued, and nobody admitted being wrong. What likely occurred?
A. The Federal Trade Commission issued a consent order, obliging the hotel to implement changes
B. Based on EU legislation, the Federal Trade Commission is allowing the hotel to comply voluntarily
C. The hotel and the Federal Trade Commission entered into a consent decree
D. A contract between the hotel and the Federal Trade Commission has been signed

15. A disgruntled guest takes the matter to court. Which of the following laws likely applies and makes this possible?
A. The Gramm-Leach-Bliley Act
B. The Health Insurance Portability and Accountability Act
C. The California Consumer Privacy Act
D. The Family Educational Rights and Privacy Act

16. During the recruitment procedure for a job you applied for at another hotel chain in California, you receive a rejection. Which of the following is most likely true?
A. You receive a copy of the investigative consumer report, regardless of whether you waived that right
B. If the organization is based in New York, you are allowed to object to the rejection in front of a committee if personal information was gathered from an external source
C. An organization is required to disclose if a social media search was used during the recruitment process
D. Since employment at will is the basis for employment, there are no privacy restrictions

17. The hotel in California collects personal information in the course of its guest registration process. Which of the following is not required before selling the personal information to a third party?
A. Provide notification to the guest
B. Provide the guest with the opportunity to opt out
C. Provide the guest with a copy of the personal information in a 'portable' format
D. Provide the opportunity to restrict the hotel from selling the personal information

18. A person's browser history can be quite revealing since, for example, it can be inferred whether a person has a certain disease or illness. What is the protection thereof?
A. Information privacy
B. Bodily privacy
C. Territorial privacy
D. Communications privacy

19. A search warrant lowers which category of privacy first?
A. Bodily privacy
B. Information privacy
C. Communication privacy
D. Territorial privacy

20. Which country's tradition of privacy was built into the U.S. Constitution?
A. The British
B. The German
C. The Dutch
D. The Portuguese

21. Which of the following is the most explicit example of the Fair Information Privacy Practice choice and consent principle?
A. Declare having read the privacy notice
B. Clear pictograms on a website indicating the functions
C. Opt-out
D. Opt-in

22. Which of the following is the most likely risk for a consumer when encountering a trust mark?
A. The trust mark having expired, and the consumer not being able to rely on it
B. The organization having illegally placed the trust mark on its website
C. Consumer responsibilities being waived
D. Presuming all his/her personal information will be handled in accordance with his/her expectations

23. Legislation from the European Union contains strict requirements regarding the information to provide before processing personal information. Which of the following is most likely allowed before showing a privacy notice?
A. Placing functional cookies
B. Using a clear GIF file
C. Placing a tracking cookie
D. Storing the IP-address' activity

24. Privacy notices can take many forms. Which of the following is not an example of a timely privacy notice?
A. A notice with information about photos being taken when entering a comedy festival
B. A notice before being allowed on a website
C. An attachment to a contract
D. A notice regarding how your personal information will be used when you receive a notification of an upcoming audit

25. In which of the following documents are you least likely going to find the retention period of the personal information in your organization?
A. A data flow diagram
B. A data inventory
C. A data deletion schedule
D. The relevant legislation

26. Organizations can experience the General Data Protection Regulation as bothersome. Which of the following is the least effective strategy to prevent the General Data Protection Regulation from being applicable?
A. Use a .com address, in English language and only allow payment in American dollar
B. Only offer your services to American citizens
C. Refuse your services to immigrants from the European Union
D. Do not ship outside the U.S.

27. Which of the following is the best example of data classification?
A. Conducting a privacy assessment
B. A data processing agreement
C. Binding Corporate Rules
D. Metadata

28. Which of the following is least important when determining which privacy laws apply?
A. The data subjects targeted
B. The location of the organization
C. The personal information's retention period
D. The number of data subjects

29. If a multinational organization mishandles the personal information of a data subject in the European Union, which of the following is most likely the case?
A. The organization will be fined a percentage of its global annual revenue
B. The data subject will have to rely on an applicable U.S. law
C. Binding Corporate Rules need to be in place before the data subject can do anything
D. The data subject can sue for damages

Use this case for the next four questions:
A global retailer has stores all over the world. The retailer sells shoes, from several different brands, both online and through their physical locations. All main brands are available in the shop, as well as the retailer's own line of shoes.

The collection in the physical stores is smaller than the collection online. However, the physical stores sell exclusive shoes at times. The shoes cannot be reserved, but customers can take part in a lottery to win the chance to reserve the exclusive shoes. For those not lucky enough to win the lottery, the only option left is to camp out in front of one of the physical stores. This has led to long lines in the past, which the retailer sees as free advertising.

Online there is the possibility to try on shoes, which is a feature the retailer is quite proud of. The process involves the customer uploading the dimensions of his/her foot, measured as accurately as possible. This allows the retailer to determine the levels of comfort of the shoes, and project the shoe in the correct size on a photo uploaded by the customer.

Another form of innovation the retailer uses is in its physical stores. This involves a sound being emitted in the store, and the customers' phones will intercept and interpret the signal through a certain social media application. The social media company will then know its user is in the retailer's store and can advertise more accurately. This benefits the retailer as well because the social media company allows the retailer to advertise on the social media page of users with similar interests.

30. The retailer has collected the personal information of many customers using its online fitting room. Which of the following is the least valid legal consideration for deleting the customers' personal information?
A. The location of storage space
B. The security of storage space
C. The applicable legislation
D. The cost of storage space

31. The retailer also has stores in the European Union. What would be an issue with using the audio beacon in its locations in the European Union?
A. The Data Protection Authority will need to approve the practice prior to implementation
B. A privacy notice needs to be provided, which can prove difficult
C. Binding Corporate Rules will need to be in place
D. A data protection impact assessment needs to be performed prior to implementation

32. The company operates in an industry that creates its own comprehensive rules. What is this an example of?
A. The comprehensive model
B. The sectoral model
C. The co-regulatory model
D. The self-regulation model

33. The company has a trust mark on its website. Which of the following is most likely the case?
A. The company does not collect personal information that users do not consent to
B. The company is compliant with all relevant privacy laws
C. The company applied for a specific trust mark, met the requirements, and got approved
D. A privacy program was fully implemented, and as a result, the company can show a trust mark on its website

34. When collecting personal information, which of the following is the most important consideration?
A. Whether you will need to conduct a privacy risk assessment
B. Whether you have the required storage space
C. Whether there is a privacy officer
D. Whether you actually need the personal information

35. Which of the following is not an example of the internet of things?
A. A smartwatch
B. Modern cars
C. Software as a service
D. A fridge streaming its content

36. Which of the following is least important for browser fingerprinting?
A. Tracking cookies
B. Font size
C. Browser type
D. General settings

37. Which of the following best describes a layered privacy notice?
A. A notice delivered at the right moment
B. A notice in the form of internationally recognized symbols
C. A notice with only the relevant requested information
D. A notice with the contact details of both the privacy officer and the data protection officer

38. Which of the following is not true regarding data retention under the Fair and Accurate Credit Transactions Act?
A. Disposal increases protection against identity theft
B. Users of credit reports need to dispose of both paper and electronic versions of the consumer reports
C. Organizations issuing consumer reports must take "reasonable measures to protect against unauthorized access or use of the information in connection with its disposal"
D. There is no responsibility with the consumer regarding disposal of the consumer report

39. Many websites display a seal, indicating recognition of privacy practices by another organization. When you come across a seal recognized by the Federal Trade Commission, for which law is that most likely?
A. The Children's Online Privacy Protection Act
B. The Fair and Accurate Credit Transactions Act
C. The Controlling the Assault of Non-Solicited Pornography And Marketing Act
D. The Gramm-Leach-Bliley Act

40. The Federal Trade Commission can allow organizations to enter into a consent decree. Which of the following policies contains the limit of enforcement of consent decrees?
A. The Enforcement Policy
B. The Consent Decree Notice
C. The Sunset Policy
D. The Federal Trade Commission Privacy Handbook

41. Which type of privacy enforcement actions are the largest part of the Federal Trade Commission's privacy law enforcement work?
A. Unfair and deceptive practices
B. Tort cases
C. Civil cases
D. General Data Protection Regulation enforcement

42. For which of the following does the Federal Trade Commission not have rule-making power?
A. The Children's Online Privacy Protection Act
B. The Health Insurance Portability and Accountability Act
C. The Telemarketing Sales Rule
D. The Controlling the Assault of Non-Solicited Pornography And Marketing Act

43. Which of the following is true regarding the outcome of an administrative trial?
A. The outcome can be appealed to the five commissioners
B. The decision can be appealed to the federal district court
C. The outcome can be ignored if the company prefers a consent decree
D. The outcome can be ignored if the case involves user consent

44. Which of the following is false regarding compliance with orders issued by the Federal Trade Commission?
A. Each violation is a separate offense
B. Each day of non-compliance is a separate offense
C. There is no redress for consumers harmed
D. If a company does not respond to the order, there can be additional penalties

45. Which of the following is likely false regarding privacy notices?
A. It can lead to deceptive practices
B. It can lead to contract breaches
C. It can lead to unfair practices
D. It can lead to violations of legal requirements

46. Your organization is subject to the same law under which the Office of Civil Rights entered into a settlement agreement with Anthem for $16 million. Which law is this?
A. The Health Insurance Portability and Accountability Act
B. The Health Information Technology for Economic and Clinical Health Act
C. The Children's Online Privacy Protection Act
D. The California Online Privacy Protection Act

47. Under Washington's HB1149, financial institutions can recover the costs of having to reissue credit cards if a data processor is the cause of a breach. Which of the following is an exception?
A. The data processor is certified as PCI-compliant
B. The data was encrypted at the time of the breach
C. The credit card owners signed a waiver
D. The breach was communicated without undue delay

48. Which of the following is false regarding business associates as mentioned in The Health Information Technology for Economic and Clinical Health Act?
A. Business associates can be compared to data processors under the General Data Protection Regulation
B. The Health Insurance Portability and Accountability Act applies to business associates
C. Business associates can be held to stricter requirements than those of the Health Insurance Portability and Accountability Act
D. There is no requirement for a business associate to protect information received from non-covered entities

Use this case for the next three questions:

A large supermarket chain in the U.S. has a popular loyalty program. Customers can sign up for a loyalty card and can either use it as is or link their name and email address to it in order to receive personalized discounts. For some customers, it is the reason they shop at this supermarket chain, and they only purchase the discounted items.

The supermarket has collected a wealth of information through this loyalty program, such as what people buy, whether they pay cash or by card, and whether they use coupons. In the past, this was information the supermarket chain could only collect in case the customer paid with a credit card since it could link all purchases made with a single credit card. However, not all customers used a credit card, and the customers who did use a credit card did not always use the same card.

Based on the patterns detected in the lists of items purchased by the individual customers, the supermarket chain organizes the supermarket in the most profitable way, making the items easy to find and placing them next to items that the customers are also likely to buy.

When it comes to those customers who linked the loyalty program card to their name and email, the supermarket chain has been able to create profiles of the type of customers it has, and adjusted its marketing strategy accordingly. For example, the supermarket chain was able to link the email address to the social media pages of the persons and in that way was able to see what the most likely commonalities between its customers were. It then incorporated that into the themes of its advertising, resulting in more effective TV commercials.

Security is important to the supermarket chain, as the supermarket chain rightfully realized that a security incident would be disastrous. It therefore appointed a Chief Information Security Officer and has reserved a significant budget for the prevention of security incidents. Privacy, however, is not too high on the supermarket chain's list of priorities, and the Chief Information Security Officer has been told privacy is also his responsibility and no dedicated privacy officer will be hired.

49. In order to perform its analyses, the supermarket chain removes the names and adds a number instead. The original list is kept separately. What is this called?
A. Anonymization
B. Aggregation
C. Encryption
D. Pseudonymization

50. The supermarket chain uses consumer reports in its pre-employment screening process, which the disposal rule requires disposal of. Which of the following is least likely a suitable method of disposal?
A. Pulverizing
B. Compressing
C. Erasing
D. Hiring a document destruction contractor

51. In case the supermarket chain uses a cloud storage provider, what is the role of the supermarket chain under the General Data Protection Regulation?
A. The supermarket chain is a data processor
B. The supermarket chain is a data controller
C. The supermarket chain is a data subject
D. The supermarket chain is a transfer party

52. The Health Insurance Portability and Accountability Act concerns 'covered entities.' Which of the following is least likely considered a covered entity?
A. A university hospital
B. Third-party organizations handling personal health information
C. A research institute handling medical data
D. A general practitioner

53. Which of the following is least likely to bring an enforcement action in relation to medical data?
A. The Department of Health and Human Services
B. The Federal Trade Commission
C. The Department of Justice
D. State attorneys general

54. After a data breach involving personal information, an organization is required to notify affected individuals. In a certain case, an organization is not required to provide a written notice to the affected parties, which of the following is most likely the case?
A. The data breach involved a very large number of individuals
B. The organization does not have the financial means
C. The organization has filed for bankruptcy
D. The data breach involves only parties that are outside of the U.S.

55. Under which other name is the Financial Services Modernization Act of 1999 also known?
A. The Fair and Accurate Credit Transactions Act
B. The Gramm-Leach-Bliley Act
C. The Fair Credit Reporting Act
D. The red flag rule

56. Which of the following is the best example of a consumer reporting agency?
A. A bank reporting on its customers
B. A data broker selling personal information
C. The Department of Justice
D. A person compiling a consumer report

57. The Fair Credit Reporting Act contains requirements for consumer reports. Which of the following is not a main requirement for a consumer report?
A. Third-party data must be appropriately accurate, current, and complete
B. The consumer reports may only be used for permissible purposes
C. Consumers must receive notice when third-party data is used in a negative decision
D. Consumers must have access to their consumer reports and the opportunity to redact them

58. Which of the following is least likely to bring enforcement action for violations of the Fair Credit Reporting Act?
A. The Federal Trade Commission
B. The Consumer Financial Protection Bureau
C. The Federal Communications Commission
D. State attorneys general

59. Under the Family Educational Rights and Privacy Act, which of the following is false regarding directory information?
A. Educational institutions are free to determine what they consider directory information
B. A student's address can be part of the directory information
C. A student's identification number can, in certain cases, be part of directory information
D. Social security numbers cannot be included in directory information

60. Directory information is generally information made accessible to others in a directory. Which of the following is most likely true about student numbers?
A. Student numbers are never included in directory information
B. Student numbers are not included in directory information if they can lead to access to records
C. The institute has no freedom to include student numbers in directory information
D. If the student is a tax dependent, his/her parents can opt to include the student number in the directory information

61. Under the Family Educational Rights and Privacy Act, which of the following may never be used as directory information?
A. Student number
B. Address
C. Phone number
D. Social security number

62. The No Child Left Behind Act provides privacy protection supplementing the Protection of Pupil Rights Amendment Act. Which type of data did this concern?
A. Political affiliations
B. Survey data
C. Religious parties
D. Income data

63. Which of the following is not included in the Controlling the Assault of Non-Solicited Pornography And Marketing Act email principles?
A. An opt-in mechanism
B. No deceptive subject lines
C. Information about the sending organization
D. No false or misleading header

64. Telemarketers do not always follow the rules. In tort law, which tort will most likely be used if it concerns telemarketers?
A. Intentional Infliction of Emotional Distress
B. Breach of Duty
C. Causation
D. Intrusion on seclusion

65. Which of the following is required to be disclosed during a telemarketing call?
A. The identity of the seller
B. The right to hang up
C. The right to object to the phone call
D. The option of being included in the National Do Not Call Registry

Use this case for the next three questions:
Heritage has become increasingly important to people over the last few years. People care about who their ancestors are, mostly because it makes for interesting conversation, or makes them feel special. An entire industry has developed to meet the demand, and there are now several providers of DNA testing that result in a somewhat accurate determination of ancestry.

The company behind the largest website for DNA testing has a variety of different purposes for the DNA it receives. It does not reveal all the tests performed on the DNA users submit, nor does it intend to link the information gained from additional testing to the individuals in question. It is the company's understanding that as long as no name is linked to the information generated, it does not concern personal information.

Despite the company's good intentions, a database with test results is leaked. For a few hundred dollars, you can buy the list on the dark web and see if anyone you know has a certain origin, but surprisingly also whether that person has a genetic predisposition to certain diseases. The leak became a huge global scandal, and a plethora of lawsuits ensued. It ruined the company, and its services are no longer available.

One of the extra tests the company performed was in collaboration with a local university's medical faculty. The evolution of disease based on heritage and migration was being researched, leading to potentially valuable information for policymakers. After the leak, the company had to stop providing information to the local university's medical faculty.

66. Which of the following can be said of the company performing undisclosed tests on the customers' DNA?
A. This concerns a deceptive trade practice
B. This concerns a breach of contract
C. This concerns a privacy notice violation
D. This constitutes an unfair trade practice

67. The company uses a postal service to ship the results to the customer. Under the General Data Protection Regulation, what can the role of the postal service likely be called?
A. The postal service is likely a data controller
B. The postal service is likely a data processor
C. The postal service is likely a data subject
D. The postal service is likely a data transfer party

68. The company has recently experienced a decrease in security incidents. Which of the following is most likely the cause?
A. New hard drives
B. A different cloud provider
C. Employee training
D. Better compression technology

69. When is a call considered abandoned?
A. When you hear nothing the first second of the call
D. When you hear chewing noises the moment you pick up the phone
C. When you are on the DNC list but still get called
D. When an automated welcome message is the first thing you hear, interrupted mid-way by a live person

70. When is sending an unsolicited commercial email not prohibited by the Controlling the Assault of Non-Solicited Pornography And Marketing Act?
A. When the recipient has opted out ten days ago
B. When the subject line can easily be interpreted differently
C. When the email contains no return address
D. When there is no clear indication that it concerns a commercial message

71. A person may obtain information from a bank through a search warrant. When must the customer be notified?
A. No later than 30 days after issuing the warrant
B. No later than 7 days after issuing the warrant
C. No later than 90 days after issuing the warrant
D. No later than 120 days after issuing the warrant

72. Privacy notices can contain statements that personal information will not be disclosed to third parties. If personal information is disclosed, which of the following is least likely true?
A. The Gramm-Leach-Bliley Act required an opt-in
B. It concerns a deceptive trade practice
C. The Children's Online Privacy Protection Act requires and opt-in
D. The Health Insurance Portability and Accountability Act required an opt-in

73. The Cybersecurity Information Sharing Act became law in 2015. Which of the following is least likely established by the Cybersecurity Information Sharing Act?
A. There will be a reduction in privacy violations
B. There will be an improvement in cybersecurity
C. There will be an improvement in privacy
D. There will be a reduction in security incidents

74. You request your personal information from the U.S. government, as allowed by a relevant law. Which law provides private right of action in case your personal information request is incorrectly denied?
A. The General Data Protection Regulation
B. The Judicial Redress Act
C. The Children's Online Privacy Protection Act
D. The USA PATRIOT Act

75. Court records are often published online. Which of the following personal information is least likely taken out before publishing court records?
A. A young offender's personal information
B. The debts of the accused
C. The websites visited by the offender
D. Details of the illness of the offender

76. Data retention programs are important and can help e-discovery. Which of the following is the least important part of a data retention program?
A. Determining the storage medium
B. Determining which documents/files to include
C. Determining the retention period
D. Taking into account the Sedona Conference guidelines

77. There are a number of federal privacy laws in the U.S. which provide privacy protection. Which of the following was the first national privacy law?
A. The Fair and Accurate Credit Transactions Act
B. The Children's Online Privacy Protection Act
C. The Controlling the Assault of Non-Solicited Pornography And Marketing Act
D. The Fair Credit Reporting Act

78. In the U.S., employees are generally employed under employment at will. Which of the following can provide the greatest privacy protection for an employee?
A. Health and safety requirements
B. State law
C. Non-discrimination laws
D. A contract

79. Which of the following is least likely a privacy risk of a bring your own device policy?
A. The company accidentally collects sensitive personal information it is not allowed to collect
B. Unauthorized access of personal information on the company network after opening a malicious email attachment
C. Company data floats around on personal devices, regardless of the data's classification
D. If a company is obliged to comply with a request to delete personal information, it can become overly complicated

80. An organization is looking to hire a Greek-speaking employee and takes out an advertisement in a newspaper in Greece. Which of the following background screening level is the maximum allowed for a remote office job?
A. Level 1 – conduct a job interview
B. Level 2 – conduct a psychometric test
C. Level 3 – conduct a polygraph test
D. Level 4 – require a blood sample

81. The Investigative Consumer Reporting Agency Act is stricter than the Fair Credit Reporting Act as regards investigative consumer reports. Which of the following is not required to be disclosed under the Investigative Consumer Reporting Agency Act?
A. The telephone number of the investigative consumer reporting agency
B. The fact that a report may be obtained
C. The email address of the investigative consumer report agency
D. What the permissible purpose of the report is

82. Video surveillance can be quite invasive. Which of the following is a way for video surveillance to fall outside the scope of federal records and stored-record statutes?
A. If the unions agree to the surveillance
B. If an employer uses closed-circuit television without sound
C. If the employer performs a privacy risk assessment prior to commencing surveillance
D. If the employer has not employed staff based on a contract

Use this case for the next two questions:
Allergens have become of increasing importance with the growing population since companies will try to widen their customer base and virtue signal how well they take care of their customers' needs. This has led to companies weighing revenue against inclusiveness.

A company producing artisanal cookies has decided to explore whether it would lose or gain customers if it changed its recipes to take into account allergies, and specifically which allergies it would have to take into account to become most profitable. The option of an extra product line with solely allergen-free cookies was also on the table, although this would entail setting up a new production facility so the different product lines cannot contaminate the allergen-free cookies.

The company has no idea how to approach the situation. At first, a survey was placed on the company's website. However, this came back with mostly useless responses, since the company's existing customers were obviously not allergic to any of the current ingredients. Then, the company approached a social media company. The social media company had access to the profiles it created for its users, including any allergens, which it derived from the content posted, shared, and liked by the user. According to the social media company, the information they provided has a 95% accuracy rate.

No personal information was sent to the artisanal cookie company, only an overview of the allergens and the percentage of users of the social media company that likely was allergic to these allergens was provided. In addition, the information was further divided into which customers were likely to buy cookies, and which were likely to pay extra for artisanal cookies. Lastly, the geographical distribution was provided, so it can be seen where the allergens have the biggest negative impact.

83. The social media company knows it has valuable and sensitive personal information and has created procedures with security practices. What are these procedures?
A. Technical security
B. Physical security
C. Organizational security
D. Administrative security

84. Which of the following is true regarding the disclosure when the cookie company calls a recent new customer, considering the Telemarketing Sales Rule?
A. If the intent is to evaluate customer satisfaction and potentially sell more, disclosure is not required
B. Even if no sales are intended to be made, disclosure is required
C. Disclosure is always required, especially if there is a prior business relationship
D. If sales are potentially going to be made, disclosure needs to happen at the beginning of the call

85. Which of the following best describes how state law is created?
A. The governor passes the bill, and the state legislature signs it into law
B. The state legislature passes the bill, and the governor signs it into law
C. The state attorney general passes the bill, and the governor signs it into law
D. The state legislature passes the bill, and the state attorney general signs it into law

86. Which state law explicitly excludes web hosting services?
A. The Delaware Online Privacy and Protection Act
B. The California Privacy Rights Act
C. Washington Biometric Privacy law HB 1493
D. Nevada SB 538

87. Which of the following is not required by the Delaware Online Privacy and Protection Act?
A. Websites must have a process for informing users of changes in the privacy policy
B. Websites are not allowed to advertise tanning beds to anyone younger than 18 years
C. Websites are forbidden to track users
D. Users can request changes to their personal information

88. The California Consumer Privacy Act grants consumers certain rights. Which of the following is not a likely result of the rights granted under the California Consumer Privacy Act?
A. The consumer cannot be subject to higher prices after opting out of his/her personal information being sold
B. The consumer can request a copy of his/her personal information free of charge
C. The consumer can pursue private civil action
D. The consumer can forbid personal information is sent to third parties

89. Which of the following is required under the California Electronic Communications and Privacy Act?
A. The Fourth Amendment of the U.S. Constitution provides roughly similar protection
B. It pertains to all personal information of Californians
C. It pertains to all personal information stored in California
D. Law enforcement officials need a warrant to search a Californian's web browsing history

90. Which of the following is most likely going to reduce the risk of non-compliance with state privacy law?
A. Identify and delete all assigned unique identifiers to the organization's customers
B. Ensure customer bank account numbers are deleted after a transaction has been completed
C. Hiring a privacy officer
D. Identify and delete all social security numbers the organization has collected

Answer key exam 1:

1A, 2C, 3C, 4B, 5D, 6B, 7A, 8B, 9A, 10D, 11B, 12B, 13A, 14C, 15C, 16A, 17C, 18A, 19D, 20A, 21D, 22D, 23A, 24A, 25A, 26C, 27D, 28C, 29D, 30D, 31B, 32D, 33C, 34D, 35C, 36A, 37C, 38C, 39A, 40C, 41A, 42B, 43A, 44C, 45C, 46A, 47B, 48D, 49D, 50B, 51B, 52C, 53A, 54A, 55B, 56D, 57D, 58C, 59A, 60B, 61D, 62B, 63A, 64D, 65A, 66D, 67B, 68C, 69D, 70A, 71C, 72A, 73A, 74B, 75C, 76A, 77D, 78D, 79B, 80A, 81C, 82B, 83D, 84D, 85B, 86A, 87C, 88D, 89D, 90D

Correct answers and explanations for exam 1:

1. Which of the following is false regarding state legislative bodies in the U.S.?
A. All states have two legislative bodies (correct)
B. Not all states have multiple legislative bodies
C. A percentage of states have two legislative body
D. All except for one state have multiple legislative bodies
Explanation:
Nebraska has a single legislative body called the *Nebraska Legislature.* Therefore, option A is false. All other states have two legislative bodies, also called *bicameral legislatures.*

2. Which of the following entities creates administrative laws?
A. The senate
B. The house of representatives
C. The Federal Trade Commission (correct)
D. The judicial branch
Explanation:
Administrative laws are rules set by the executive branch. The Federal Trade Commission is the only correct option since it is the only option part of the executive branch.

3. Administrative law is different from case law. Where is administrative law documented?
A. The Federal Trade Commission guidelines
B. The Federal Communications Commission guidelines
C. The Code of Federal Regulations (correct)
D. An executive order
Explanation:
The Code of Federal Regulations is where administrative law is commonly documented. The other options are less likely. For the exam, you should remember that the Code of Federal Regulations contains administrative law.

4. If, at some point, the U.S. Constitution gets amended, which requirement has been met?
A. The president has issued an executive order
B. Three-quarters of the states have ratified the amendment (correct)
C. Congress has voted, and the amendment received a majority vote
D. The president did not execute a veto
Explanation:
In order to amend the U.S. Constitution, Congress first needs to approve the amendment. After that, 38 out of 50 states (which is three-quarters) will need to ratify the amendment. Option C is also important, but the part that is missing is that a two-thirds majority is required.

5. Judges in the judicial branch are appointed by the president. Which of the following do not serve until death, resignation, or impeachment?
A. Supreme court judges
B. Circuit court judges
C. District court judges
D. None of the answers are correct (correct)
Explanation:
All judges serve until death, resignation, or impeachment. Therefore, option D is the correct answer.

6. Which of the following signs proposed bills into federal law?
A. The house of representatives
B. The executive branch (correct)
C. The senate
D. Congress
Explanation:
The president signs proposed bills into law. This is federal law, and the president is part of the executive branch. Therefore, option B is correct.

7. When a legal decision includes the term 'stare decisis', what is likely the case?
A. The decision is (partly) based on a previous legal decision (correct)
B. The legal decision is setting a precedent
C. It concerns a decision at the federal level only
D. It concerns a decision at the state level only
Explanation:
Stare decisis is when a decision is based on a previous legal decision, either at the same level of court or at a different level court. Option A is therefore correct. Option B is related, but for future legal decisions since stare decisis is the use of a precedent and not setting one. Options C and D are incorrect because stare decisis can be at any level court.

8. A court does not always have the authority to hear cases in a particular area of the law. In that case, which of the following is missing?
A. Preemption of the relevant state law
B. Subject matter jurisdiction (correct)
C. Preemption of the relevant federal law
D. A contract that covers the subject in question
Explanation:
Not all courts have jurisdiction over all subject matter, which is referred to as subject matter jurisdiction. There is a chance this is not covered in your study materials, so be prepared for questions for which you will have to make an educated guess.

9. Which of the following is least likely true regarding case law?
A. Case law is based on common principles found in previous court cases (correct)
B. Case law is used to resolve civil and criminal disputes
C. Applying case law is a form of stare decisis
D. Case law decisions are binding on subordinate courts
Explanation:
Option A describes common law, and therefore is the correct answer. The other options are true for case law.

10. Contracts can be a source of privacy protection. Which of the following is least likely true regarding contracts?
A. A fine issued for speeding after signing for receipt is not a contract
B. If only one party offers something of value, it is not a contract
C. You cannot enter into a contract without intending to be bound by it
D. You can sell your house and agree on the terms verbally, but having the terms in writing takes precedence (correct)
Explanation:
All are true, except some contracts are required to be in writing. Selling a house is one of the contracts which is required to be in writing. Perhaps this is a useless fact, not related to privacy, but questions like this can appear on the exam. Do not stress too much about the details though, as you can still pass if you miss a few questions.

11. Which court only has jurisdiction over specific U.S. states?
A. State court
B. Circuit court (correct)
C. U.S. supreme court
D. European Court of Justice
Explanation:
A circuit court has jurisdiction over several *specific* states. The state court pertains just to a single state, and the question here is plural. Therefore, B is the correct answer.

12. Preponderance of evidence is most relevant in which of the following situations?
A. The Federal Trade Commission entered into a consent decree with an organization to fix the organization's privacy issues
B. A person suing a company for damages because of the mishandling of personal information (correct)
C. A privacy dispute in which a privacy officer mediates
D. In case there is strict liability
Explanation:
Preponderance of evidence is demonstrating that there is a more than 50% chance the party's claim is correct. This is applicable in civil cases, and option B provides the clearest example of a civil case.

13. Tracking cookies can track which website a user has visited. Which law does that most likely violate?

A. The General Data Protection Regulation (correct)

B. The Fair and Accurate Credit Transactions Act

C. The Controlling the Assault of Non-Solicited Pornography And Marketing Act

D. The Health Insurance Portability and Accountability Act

Explanation:

The General Data Protection Regulation is quite strict and prohibits the processing of personal information without a legal basis. Placing a tracking cookie generally requires permission, which is not likely given in case a user is asked to let the website know which websites he/she is visiting. The other three options do not provide significant protection against tracking cookies, mostly because it is out of their scope. Option A is the correct answer.

Use this case for the next three questions:

In recent years many new hotels opened in California. You always had the ambition of working in the hospitality industry, and with your newly acquired privacy certification, you are going to give it a shot. After searching through all the job vacancy websites, you select the ten most interesting vacancies and send in your application.

Several of the hotels invite you for an interview, and one hotel even asks you to send in a photo of yourself prior to a final invitation to the interview. You find sending a photograph a little intrusive, and also likely to hurt your chances, so you decline and, in an effort to be clever, you add the message 'I would not be a good privacy officer if I obliged to your request, as any data gathered from the photo is irrelevant for assessing my suitability for the vacant position'. Eventually, you are offered a position, and start work at your second-choice hotel, as the privacy officer.

During your first week you familiarize yourself with the hotel's practices concerning the collection and use of personal information. Guests generally book a room through one of the well-known booking websites. This process includes the booking website transferring guest information, such as name, date of birth, credit card number, and address. The personal information is stored on the hotel's server, which is accessible from all other locations of the hotel chain.

When a guest arrives, additional personal information is requested. This concerns a copy of a form of ID and the information concerning the other guests in the room. All guests receive a personal code for the Wi-Fi, which allows the hotel to keep track of all guests' internet activity. The hotel does this in order to pinpoint which guest is responsible in case any illegal activities take place, and the internet activity is stored for six months.

14. After the hotel has been accused of overly invasive privacy practices, the Federal Trade Commission and the organization agree on changes to be implemented. No fine is issued, and nobody admitted being wrong. What likely occurred?
A. The Federal Trade Commission issued a consent order, obliging the hotel to implement changes
B. Based on EU legislation, the Federal Trade Commission is allowing the hotel to comply voluntarily
C. The hotel and the Federal Trade Commission entered into a consent decree (correct)
D. A contract between the hotel and the Federal Trade Commission has been signed
Explanation:
This situation clearly describes a consent decree (not a consent order). Therefore, option C is the correct answer. The exam will have the occasional easy question like this one.

15. A disgruntled guest takes the matter to court. Which of the following laws likely applies and makes this possible?
A. The Gramm-Leach-Bliley Act
B. The Health Insurance Portability and Accountability Act
C. The California Consumer Privacy Act (correct)
D. The Family Educational Rights and Privacy Act
Explanation:
From both the subject matter and the geographical location, you should have concluded that the California Consumer Privacy Act is more likely to apply than the other options.

16. During the recruitment procedure for a job you applied for at another hotel chain in California, you receive a rejection. Which of the following is most likely true?
A. You receive a copy of the investigative consumer report, regardless of whether you waived that right (correct)
B. If the organization is based in New York, you are allowed to object to the rejection in front of a committee if personal information was gathered from an external source
C. An organization is required to disclose if a social media search was used during the recruitment process
D. Since employment at will is the basis for employment, there are no privacy restrictions
Explanation:
The Investigative Consumer Reporting Agency Act of California allows you to receive a copy of the investigative consumer report, even if you have waived that right. Option C could also be correct, but only in case of rejection.

17. The hotel in California collects personal information in the course of its guest registration process. Which of the following is not required before selling the personal information to a third party?
A. Provide notification to the guest
B. Provide the guest with the opportunity to opt out
C. Provide the guest with a copy of the personal information in a 'portable' format (correct)
D. Provide the opportunity to restrict the hotel from selling the personal information
Explanation:
It is not required to provide the personal information to the guest before selling it. Opting out, notification, and the opportunity to restrict are required.

18. A person's browser history can be quite revealing since, for example, it can be inferred whether a person has a certain disease or illness. What is the protection thereof?
A. Information privacy (correct)
B. Bodily privacy
C. Territorial privacy
D. Communications privacy
Explanation:
Here it does not concern bodily privacy, since the body is not invaded (only potential information about the body), nor is it communications privacy since browser history does not constitute communication (content transmitted to the website is not part of the browser history). Therefore, it most likely concerns information privacy.

19. A search warrant lowers which category of privacy first?
A. Bodily privacy
B. Information privacy
C. Communication privacy
D. Territorial privacy (correct)
Explanation:
Although the Fourth Amendment possibly applies, territorial privacy is the most likely category of privacy lowered. Your home or property (territory) is being entered and searched. Whatever is found can lead to affecting information and communication privacy, but territorial privacy was affected first.

20. Which country's tradition of privacy was built into the U.S. Constitution?
A. The British (correct)
B. The German
C. The Dutch
D. The Portuguese
Explanation:
This is perhaps a useless thing to know, but the British tradition of privacy was built into the U.S. Constitution.

21. Which of the following is the most explicit example of the Fair Information Privacy Practice choice and consent principle?
A. Declare having read the privacy notice
B. Clear pictograms on a website indicating the functions
C. Opt-out
D. Opt-in (correct)
Explanation:
The options all provide examples of choice to some extent. Opting in and opting out are examples of consent. Opting in is the most explicit version of consent since the user will need to actively indicate he/she is opting in. Opting out requires an action if the user does not consent, and is, therefore, less explicit consent than opting in.

22. Which of the following is the most likely risk for a consumer when encountering a trust mark?
A. The trust mark having expired, and the consumer not being able to rely on it
B. The organization having illegally placed the trust mark on its website
C. Consumer responsibilities being waived
D. Presuming all his/her personal information will be handled in accordance with his/her expectations (correct)
Explanation:
Consumers see a trust mark and presume their personal information is handled a certain way. This can lead to a false sense of security, especially since consumers do not know exactly what a certain trust mark means. It can therefore be the case that the company still uses the personal information for a purpose that the consumer did not expect, such as transferring it to third parties. Requirements of a trust mark are specific and are not necessarily aligned with consumer expectations, so you should still read the privacy notice.

23. Legislation from the European Union contains strict requirements regarding the information to provide before processing personal information. Which of the following is most likely allowed before showing a privacy notice?
A. Placing functional cookies (correct)
B. Using a clear GIF file
C. Placing a tracking cookie
D. Storing the IP-address' activity
Explanation:
Functional cookies are required to let a website function and do not necessarily lead to collecting or processing personal information. The other three are invasive, and will likely need consent under the General Data Protection Regulation, for which information (usually in the form of a privacy notice) will need to be provided in order to get properly informed consent. In case you did not make the connection, a clear GIF is a different name for a web beacon or tracking pixel.

24. Privacy notices can take many forms. Which of the following is not an example of a timely privacy notice?
A. A notice with information about photos being taken when entering a comedy festival (correct)
B. A notice before being allowed on a website
C. An attachment to a contract
D. A notice regarding how your personal information will be used when you receive a notification of an upcoming audit
Explanation:
Although this happens a lot in practice, posting a privacy notice at the entrance of a festival is too late. The visitor should have received the privacy notice when purchasing the ticket, so the visitor could have opted not to purchase a ticket if he/she is not comfortable with photos being taken at the festival. Now, the ticket has been purchased, and the information is no longer relevant (unless you consider wasting ticket money and time traveling to the festival reasonable).

25. In which of the following documents are you least likely going to find the retention period of the personal information in your organization?

A. A data flow diagram (correct)

B. A data inventory

C. A data deletion schedule

D. The relevant legislation

Explanation:

A data flow describes the flow of the data and does not (or at least not necessarily) have the retention period of the data. The others should have a retention period. Legislation can have specific retention periods or rules with which to determine the retention period.

26. Organizations can experience the General Data Protection Regulation as bothersome. Which of the following is the least effective strategy to prevent the General Data Protection Regulation from being applicable?

A. Use a .com address, in English language and only allow payment in American dollar

B. Only offer your services to American citizens

C. Refuse your services to immigrants from the European Union (correct)

D. Do not ship outside the U.S.

Explanation:

Option C is the least effective because when people immigrate from the European Union, they are no longer citizens of the European Union, and the General Data Protection Regulation most likely does not apply to the processing of personal information in the United States. The other options might increase your chances of not having to comply with the General Data Protection Regulation, but do not necessarily prevent it. The options are all farfetched, but the point is that for option C the General Data Protection Regulation per definition does not apply.

27. Which of the following is the best example of data classification?
A. Conducting a privacy assessment
B. A data processing agreement
C. Binding Corporate Rules
D. Metadata (correct)
Explanation:
Metadata is data about data. It can contain the classification of the data. The other options do not contain anything that classifies data, although they could specify classes of data to be used (but they do not classify data themselves).

28. Which of the following is least important when determining which privacy laws apply?
A. The data subjects targeted
B. The location of the organization
C. The personal information's retention period (correct)
D. The number of data subjects
Explanation:
Option C is the correct answer because it is the other way around. The retention period is influenced by which laws apply, but the retention period does not influence which law applies.

29. If a multinational organization mishandles the personal information of a data subject in the European Union, which of the following is most likely the case?
A. The organization will be fined a percentage of its global annual revenue
B. The data subject will have to rely on an applicable U.S. law
C. Binding Corporate Rules need to be in place before the data subject can do anything
D. The data subject can sue for damages (correct)
Explanation:
Article 82 of the General Data Protection Regulation grants the right to compensation for material or non-material damage suffered by data subjects as a result of infringements of the General Data Protection Regulation. This is not to be confused with the fines that organizations can receive.

Use this case for the next four questions:
A global retailer has stores all over the world. The retailer sells shoes, from several different brands, both online and through their physical locations. All main brands are available in the shop, as well as the retailer's own line of shoes.

The collection in the physical stores is smaller than the collection online. However, the physical stores sell exclusive shoes at times. The shoes cannot be reserved, but customers can take part in a lottery to win the chance to reserve the exclusive shoes. For those not lucky enough to win the lottery, the only option left is to camp out in front of one of the physical stores. This has led to long lines in the past, which the retailer sees as free advertising.

Online there is the possibility to try on shoes, which is a feature the retailer is quite proud of. The process involves the customer uploading the dimensions of his/her foot, measured as accurately as possible. This allows the retailer to determine the levels of comfort of the shoes, and project the shoe in the correct size on a photo uploaded by the customer.

Another form of innovation the retailer uses is in its physical stores. This involves a sound being emitted in the store, and the customers' phones will intercept and interpret the signal through a certain social media application. The social media company will then know its user is in the retailer's store and can advertise more accurately. This benefits the retailer as well because the social media company allows the retailer to advertise on the social media page of users with similar interests.

30. The retailer has collected the personal information of many customers using its online fitting room. Which of the following is the least valid legal consideration for deleting the customers' personal information?
A. The location of storage space
B. The security of storage space
C. The applicable legislation
D. The cost of storage space (correct)
Explanation:
The cost of storage is likely insignificant, and the costs have no legal consequences. Depending on the location, different laws can apply (think about storing in the European Union for example). Regarding security, certain laws require a certain level of security for certain types of personal information, hence this is an important consideration.

31. The retailer also has stores in the European Union. What would be an issue with using the audio beacon in its locations in the European Union?
A. The Data Protection Authority will need to approve the practice prior to implementation
B. A privacy notice needs to be provided, which can prove difficult (correct)
C. Binding Corporate Rules will need to be in place
D. A data protection impact assessment needs to be performed prior to implementation
Explanation:
All options could be true depending on the circumstances, but option B is correct in this case since a privacy notice needs to be provided and with the use of an audio beacon this could prove difficult.

32. The company operates in an industry that creates its own comprehensive rules. What is this an example of?
A. The comprehensive model
B. The sectoral model
C. The co-regulatory model
D. The self-regulation model (correct)
Explanation:
The industry creates its own rules, which is self-regulation. If the government was partially involved, it would have been co-regulation, and if the government made all the rules for this industry, it would have been the sectoral model.

33. The company has a trust mark on its website. Which of the following is most likely the case?
A. The company does not collect personal information that users do not consent to
B. The company is compliant with all relevant privacy laws
C. The company applied for a specific trust mark, met the requirements, and got approved (correct)
D. A privacy program was fully implemented, and as a result, the company can show a trust mark on its website
Explanation:
All that a trust mark indicates is that a third party verified that the company met certain standards. Which standards are met can vary from trust mark to trust mark, so look at the specifics of the trust mark before concluding on the organization's privacy practices.

34. When collecting personal information, which of the following is the most important consideration?
A. Whether you will need to conduct a privacy risk assessment
B. Whether you have the required storage space
C. Whether there is a privacy officer
D. Whether you actually need the personal information (correct)
Explanation:
Whether you actually need the personal information is quite an important consideration. Having personal information in your organization for which you have no use (for example, having it just in case it might be useful at some point) is not worth the risk of not complying with any laws which are applicable due to having that specific personal information.

35. Which of the following is not an example of the internet of things?
A. A smartwatch
B. Modern cars
C. Software as a service (correct)
D. A fridge streaming its content
Explanation:
All examples, except for option C, are devices connected to the internet. Option C is not an example of the internet of things, but software run from a server (which is an oversimplified description).

36. Which of the following is least important for browser fingerprinting?
A. Tracking cookies (correct)
B. Font size
C. Browser type
D. General settings
Explanation:
A tracking cookie is not a setting related to a browser. The other examples are settings of a browser, the collective of which can be used to somewhat accurately identify an individual. The collection of settings is also referred to as a browser's 'fingerprint'.

37. Which of the following best describes a layered privacy notice?
A. A notice delivered at the right moment
B. A notice in the form of internationally recognized symbols
C. A notice with only the relevant requested information (correct)
D. A notice with the contact details of both the privacy officer and the data protection officer
Explanation:
The important thing with a layered privacy notice is that it consists of different layers, which are only displayed when relevant or requested. For example, when a website offers different services, only the relevant layer for the selective service needs to be shown. Or, there is different privacy information for different steps in the procedure, and only when progressing to the next step in the process is the next layer with privacy information shown.

38. Which of the following is not true regarding data retention under the Fair and Accurate Credit Transactions Act?
A. Disposal increases protection against identity theft
B. Users of credit reports need to dispose of both paper and electronic versions of the consumer reports
C. Organizations issuing consumer reports must take "reasonable measures to protect against unauthorized access or use of the information in connection with its disposal" (correct)
D. There is no responsibility with the consumer regarding disposal of the consumer report
Explanation:
This rule concerns covered organizations, not organizations issuing consumer reports. Covered organizations here refers to organizations that use consumer reports.

39. Many websites display a seal, indicating recognition of privacy practices by another organization. When you come across a seal recognized by the Federal Trade Commission, for which law is that most likely?
A. The Children's Online Privacy Protection Act (correct)
B. The Fair and Accurate Credit Transactions Act
C. The Controlling the Assault of Non-Solicited Pornography And Marketing Act
D. The Gramm-Leach-Bliley Act
Explanation:
The Federal Trade Commission issues a seal for the Children's Online Privacy Protection Act. This is an important fact to remember because this is one of the few examples of a seal provided by the Federal Trade Commission.

40. The Federal Trade Commission can allow organizations to enter into a consent decree. Which of the following policies contains the limit of enforcement of consent decrees?
A. The Enforcement Policy
B. The Consent Decree Notice
C. The Sunset Policy (correct)
D. The Federal Trade Commission Privacy Handbook
Explanation:
The Sunset Policy contains the limit of enforcement of consent decrees. This is a useless fact, but there will be questions like this on the exam. Do not worry too much about forgetting facts, as you can sometimes guess the correct answer without actually knowing the answer.

41. Which type of privacy enforcement actions are the largest part of the Federal Trade Commission's privacy law enforcement work?
A. Unfair and deceptive practices (correct)
B. Tort cases
C. Civil cases
D. General Data Protection Regulation enforcement
Explanation:
Most privacy enforcement actions of the Federal Trade Commission concern unfair and deceptive practices. The other three are unlikely, although you might want to keep track of a possible role of the Federal Trade Commission with the development of the EU-US Privacy Shield (if any).

42. For which of the following does the Federal Trade Commission not have rule-making power?
A. The Children's Online Privacy Protection Act
B. The Health Insurance Portability and Accountability Act (correct)
C. The Telemarketing Sales Rule
D. The Controlling the Assault of Non-Solicited Pornography And Marketing Act
Explanation:
The Federal Trade Commission does not have rule-making power over the Health Insurance Portability and Accountability Act. Therefore, option B is the correct answer. It is important to note that the Federal Trade Commission does have rule-making power for the Health Information Technology for Economic and Clinical Health Act.

43. Which of the following is true regarding the outcome of an administrative trial?
A. The outcome can be appealed to the five commissioners (correct)
B. The decision can be appealed to the federal district court
C. The outcome can be ignored if the company prefers a consent decree
D. The outcome can be ignored if the case involves user consent
Explanation:
The Federal Trade Commission can start an administrative trial. The outcome can be appealed to the five commissioners. These five commissioners are the executive authority of the Federal Trade Commission, appointed by the president. Option A is therefore correct, option B comes after.

44. Which of the following is false regarding compliance with orders issued by the Federal Trade Commission?
A. Each violation is a separate offense
B. Each day of non-compliance is a separate offense
C. There is no redress for consumers harmed (correct)
D. If a company does not respond to the order, there can be additional penalties
Explanation:
All are true except for C. There can be redress for consumers harmed by an organization's privacy practices as a result of not complying with the Federal Trade Commission's orders, but a judge has to order it.

45. Which of the following is likely false regarding privacy notices?
A. It can lead to deceptive practices
B. It can lead to contract breaches
C. It can lead to unfair practices (correct)
D. It can lead to violations of legal requirements
Explanation:
If a privacy notice states false information, it is deceptive. If a privacy notice is not respected, it can be a contract breach. If the privacy notice does not contain all information legally required (or is not provided at the correct time) it can be a violation of legal requirements. A privacy notice, however, is less likely to lead to an unfair practice because the unfair practice would occur in something unavoidable an organization does with your personal information, but not which information it provides. Therefore, C is the correct answer.

46. Your organization is subject to the same law under which the Office of Civil Rights entered into a settlement agreement with Anthem for $16 million. Which law is this?
A. The Health Insurance Portability and Accountability Act (correct)
B. The Health Information Technology for Economic and Clinical Health Act
C. The Children's Online Privacy Protection Act
D. The California Online Privacy Protection Act
Explanation:
A is the correct answer. The example of Anthem should be included in your study material. For all case examples provided in your study material, analyze the principles applied and the actors involved, this should help you with questions like this one.

47. Under Washington's HB1149, financial institutions can recover the costs of having to reissue credit cards if a data processor is the cause of a breach. Which of the following is an exception?
A. The data processor is certified as PCI-compliant
B. The data was encrypted at the time of the breach (correct)
C. The credit card owners signed a waiver
D. The breach was communicated without undue delay
Explanation:
If the data was properly encrypted, it was unreadable for those without the key. It would therefore possibly not be necessary to issue a new credit card. Option A could also be correct, but only if the data processor was certified as PCI-compliant within one year of the breach, which is not specified here.

48. Which of the following is false regarding business associates as mentioned in The Health Information Technology for Economic and Clinical Health Act?
A. Business associates can be compared to data processors under the General Data Protection Regulation
B. The Health Insurance Portability and Accountability Act applies to business associates
C. Business associates can be held to stricter requirements than those of the Health Insurance Portability and Accountability Act
D. There is no requirement for a business associate to protect information received from non-covered entities (correct)
Explanation:
Even if the information is received from non-covered entities, the information needs to be protected. Option D is correct. Regarding option C, there is no preemption in this case, so there can be stricter requirements.

Use this case for the next three questions:
A large supermarket chain in the U.S. has a popular loyalty program. Customers can sign up for a loyalty card and can either use it as is or link their name and email address to it in order to receive personalized discounts. For some customers, it is the reason they shop at this supermarket chain, and they only purchase the discounted items.

The supermarket has collected a wealth of information through this loyalty program, such as what people buy, whether they pay cash or by card, and whether they use coupons. In the past, this was information the supermarket chain could only collect in case the customer paid with a credit card since it could link all purchases made with a single credit card. However, not all customers used a credit card, and the customers who did use a credit card did not always use the same card.

Based on the patterns detected in the lists of items purchased by the individual customers, the supermarket chain organizes the supermarket in the most profitable way, making the items easy to find and placing them next to items that the customers are also likely to buy.

When it comes to those customers who linked the loyalty program card to their name and email, the supermarket chain has been able to create profiles of the type of customers it has, and adjusted its marketing strategy accordingly. For example, the supermarket chain was able to link the email address to the social media pages of the persons and in that way was able to see what the most likely commonalities between its customers were. It then incorporated that into the themes of its advertising, resulting in more effective TV commercials.

Security is important to the supermarket chain, as the supermarket chain rightfully realized that a security incident would be disastrous. It therefore appointed a Chief Information Security Officer and has reserved a significant budget for the prevention of security incidents. Privacy, however, is not too high on the supermarket chain's list of priorities, and the Chief Information Security Officer has been told privacy is also his responsibility and no dedicated privacy officer will be hired.

49. In order to perform its analyses, the supermarket chain removes the names and adds a number instead. The original list is kept separately. What is this called?
A. Anonymization
B. Aggregation
C. Encryption
D. Pseudonymization (correct)
Explanation:
This is an example of pseudonymization, where the name is removed and a number, code, or other identifier is added to keep the record apart from the others. This process is reversible if a list is kept of which names correspond with which number. Pseudonymization is often used in research. Option D is correct. Anonymization would be irreversible, which is not the case here.

50. The supermarket chain uses consumer reports in its pre-employment screening process, which the disposal rule requires disposal of. Which of the following is least likely a suitable method of disposal?
A. Pulverizing
B. Compressing (correct)
C. Erasing
D. Hiring a document destruction contractor
Explanation:
Compression makes files smaller but does not destroy them. Therefore, this is not a way of disposing of files.

51. In case the supermarket chain uses a cloud storage provider, what is the role of the supermarket chain under the General Data Protection Regulation?
A. The supermarket chain is a data processor
B. The supermarket chain is a data controller (correct)
C. The supermarket chain is a data subject
D. The supermarket chain is a transfer party
Explanation:
The supermarket chain is the party in control and therefore determines what is done with the personal information and how it is done. The cloud provider stores it at the request of the supermarket chain, following the instructions of the supermarket chain, and is a data processor.

52. The Health Insurance Portability and Accountability Act concerns 'covered entities.' Which of the following is least likely considered a covered entity?
A. A university hospital
B. Third-party organizations handling personal health information
C. A research institute handling medical data (correct)
D. A general practitioner
Explanation:
An electronic reimbursement is required for the Health Insurance Portability and Accountability Act to apply. The research institute is the least likely place where electronic reimbursement takes place, and therefore the correct answer. This does not mean that the other options concern electronic reimbursements per definition, since you can pay a general practitioner in cash for example, but it concerns the least likely for this question.

53. Which of the following is least likely to bring an enforcement action in relation to medical data?
A. The Department of Health and Human Services (correct)
B. The Federal Trade Commission
C. The Department of Justice
D. State attorneys general
Explanation:
The Department of Health and Human Services works with other agencies but does not enforce. Therefore, A is the correct answer. The other options do enforce.

54. After a data breach involving personal information, an organization is required to notify affected individuals. In a certain case, an organization is not required to provide a written notice to the affected parties, which of the following is most likely the case?
A. The data breach involved a very large number of individuals (correct)
B. The organization does not have the financial means
C. The organization has filed for bankruptcy
D. The data breach involves only parties that are outside of the U.S.
Explanation:
When notifying individuals after a data breach, some legislation allows an organization not to notify the individuals if it places an undue financial burden on the organization. Of the options provided, option A is the most realistic scenario where it could be justified not to notify the affected individuals (assuming there is not an easy way of contacting them). What is missing here is the severity of the possible consequences for the data subjects, but during the exam you will have to work with the information provided in the question and make assumptions.

55. Under which other name is the Financial Services Modernization Act of 1999 also known?
A. The Fair and Accurate Credit Transactions Act
B. The Gramm-Leach-Bliley Act (correct)
C. The Fair Credit Reporting Act
D. The red flag rule
Explanation:
The Financial Services Modernization Act is also known as the Gramm-Leach-Bliley Act. This is something you either know or do not know, so this should not cost you much time on the exam. If you do not know the answer, just flag it and see if the answer comes to you later.

56. Which of the following is the best example of a consumer reporting agency?
A. A bank reporting on its customers
B. A data broker selling personal information
C. The Department of Justice
D. A person compiling a consumer report (correct)
Explanation:
A consumer reporting agency is a person or entity compiling or evaluating personal information to furnish consumer reports for a fee. Option D fits this definition best (although the fee is missing), and is therefore the correct answer.

57. The Fair Credit Reporting Act contains requirements for consumer reports. Which of the following is not a main requirement for a consumer report?
A. Third-party data must be appropriately accurate, current, and complete
B. The consumer reports may only be used for permissible purposes
C. Consumers must receive notice when third-party data is used in a negative decision
D. Consumers must have access to their consumer reports and the opportunity to redact them (correct)
Explanation:
Option D is false because consumers are only allowed to dispute their consumer reports, not redact them. Watch out for small differences like this.

58. Which of the following is least likely to bring enforcement action for violations of the Fair Credit Reporting Act?
A. The Federal Trade Commission
B. The Consumer Financial Protection Bureau
C. The Federal Communications Commission (correct)
D. State attorneys general
Explanation:
The Federal Communications Commission cannot bring enforcement action for violations of the Fair Credit Reporting Act. If you did not know the answer, perhaps you could have guessed it based on credit reporting not being related to communication.

59. Under the Family Educational Rights and Privacy Act, which of the following is false regarding directory information?
A. Educational institutions are free to determine what they consider directory information (correct)
B. A student's address can be part of the directory information
C. A student's identification number can, in certain cases, be part of directory information
D. Social security numbers cannot be included in directory information
Explanation:
There are limitations on what educational institutions can include in directory information, hence they are not 'free' to determine what they consider directory information.

60. Directory information is generally information made accessible to others in a directory. Which of the following is most likely true about student numbers?
A. Student numbers are never included in directory information
B. Student numbers are not included in directory information if they can lead to access to records (correct)
C. The institute has no freedom to include student numbers in directory information
D. If the student is a tax dependent, his/her parents can opt to include the student number in the directory information
Explanation:
Option B describes a limitation of the use of student numbers as directory information. It would be quite invasive if the student numbers are also part of the login credentials for the students, which they often are, and therefore this limitation makes sense.

61. Under the Family Educational Rights and Privacy Act, which of the following may never be used as directory information?
A. Student number
B. Address
C. Phone number
D. Social security number (correct)
Explanation:
This one goes without saying, social security numbers open up possibilities for identity theft and other malicious activities.

62. The No Child Left Behind Act provides privacy protection supplementing the Protection of Pupil Rights Amendment Act. Which type of data did this concern?
A. Political affiliations
B. Survey data (correct)
C. Religious parties
D. Income data
Explanation:
The No Child Left Behind Act concerned survey data, and more specifically it placed restrictions on the collection and disclosure of survey data.

63. Which of the following is not included in the Controlling the Assault of Non-Solicited Pornography And Marketing Act email principles?
A. An opt-in mechanism (correct)
B. No deceptive subject lines
C. Information about the sending organization
D. No false or misleading header
Explanation:
Option A is the correct answer. It should be an opt-out mechanism, not an opt-in.

64. Telemarketers do not always follow the rules. In tort law, which tort will most likely be used if it concerns telemarketers?
A. Intentional Infliction of Emotional Distress
B. Breach of Duty
C. Causation
D. Intrusion on seclusion (correct)
Explanation:
Intrusion on seclusion is the intentional intrusion in private affairs/concerns or solitude. This must be highly offensive to a reasonable person. This tort is most likely used in tort cases involving telemarketers.

65. Which of the following is required to be disclosed during a telemarketing call?
A. The identity of the seller (correct)
B. The right to hang up
C. The right to object to the phone call
D. The option of being included in the National Do Not Call Registry
Explanation:
Option A is correct, the identity of the seller needs to be disclosed during a telemarketing call.

Use this case for the next three questions:
Heritage has become increasingly important to people over the last few years. People care about who their ancestors are, mostly because it makes for interesting conversation, or makes them feel special. An entire industry has developed to meet the demand, and there are now several providers of DNA testing that result in a somewhat accurate determination of ancestry.

The company behind the largest website for DNA testing has a variety of different purposes for the DNA it receives. It does not reveal all the tests performed on the DNA users submit, nor does it intend to link the information gained from additional testing to the individuals in question. It is the company's understanding that as long as no name is linked to the information generated, it does not concern personal information.

Despite the company's good intentions, a database with test results is leaked. For a few hundred dollars, you can buy the list on the dark web and see if anyone you know has a certain origin, but surprisingly also whether that person has a genetic predisposition to certain diseases. The leak became a huge global scandal, and a plethora of lawsuits ensued. It ruined the company, and its services are no longer available.

One of the extra tests the company performed was in collaboration with a local university's medical faculty. The evolution of disease based on heritage and migration was being researched, leading to potentially valuable information for policymakers. After the leak, the company had to stop providing information to the local university's medical faculty.

66. Which of the following can be said of the company performing undisclosed tests on the customers' DNA?
A. This concerns a deceptive trade practice
B. This concerns a breach of contract
C. This concerns a privacy notice violation
D. This constitutes an unfair trade practice (correct)
Explanation:
This is most likely an unfair trade practice, as it is unfair to sneakily do other things with personal information. It would have been deceptive if the privacy notice or agreement would have specified or created the impression that no extra tests are done.

67. The company uses a postal service to ship the results to the customer. Under the General Data Protection Regulation, what can the role of the postal service likely be called?
A. The postal service is likely a data controller
B. The postal service is likely a data processor (correct)
C. The postal service is likely a data subject
D. The postal service is likely a data transfer party
Explanation:
The postal service processes the personal information (the name and address, as well as the test results) under the direction of the company. Thus, the company is ultimately the one responsible and in control (the postal service is not supposed to deviate from the instructions/agreement).

68. The company has recently experienced a decrease in security incidents. Which of the following is most likely the cause?
A. New hard drives
B. A different cloud provider
C. Employee training (correct)
D. Better compression technology
Explanation:
Of the factors listed, employees are the most likely cause of security incidents. Therefore, employee training has the biggest impact, which was what this question was really asking. All of the listed answers can have some effect on the reduction in the number (or severity) of security incidents, but employee training likely has the biggest impact.

69. When is a call considered abandoned?

A. When you hear nothing the first second of the call

D. When you hear chewing noises the moment you pick up the phone

C. When you are on the DNC list but still get called

D. When an automated welcome message is the first thing you hear, interrupted mid-way by a live person (correct)

Explanation:

A call is abandoned if you are not connected to a live person within two seconds after picking up the phone and saying 'hello'. Option D best describes this, as more than two seconds likely have passed.

70. When is sending an unsolicited commercial email not prohibited by the Controlling the Assault of Non-Solicited Pornography And Marketing Act?

A. When the recipient has opted out ten days ago (correct)

B. When the subject line can easily be interpreted differently

C. When the email contains no return address

D. When there is no clear indication that it concerns a commercial message

Explanation:

Option A is the correct answer, and it might be difficult to spot why. There is a grace period of ten <u>business</u> days, and thus when having opted out ten (calendar) days ago these ten business days have not passed yet.

71. A person may obtain information from a bank through a search warrant. When must the customer be notified?

A. No later than 30 days after issuing the warrant

B. No later than 7 days after issuing the warrant

C. No later than 90 days after issuing the warrant (correct)

D. No later than 120 days after issuing the warrant

Explanation:

The customer must be notified no later than 90 days after the warrant was issued. An exception is if a court authorizes a delay of this notification.

72. Privacy notices can contain statements that personal information will not be disclosed to third parties. If personal information is disclosed, which of the following is least likely true?
A. The Gramm-Leach-Bliley Act required an opt-in (correct)
B. It concerns a deceptive trade practice
C. The Children's Online Privacy Protection Act requires and opt-in
D. The Health Insurance Portability and Accountability Act required an opt-in
Explanation:
Only an opt-out is required to prevent disclosure to third parties under the Gramm-Leach-Bliley Act, not an opt-in.

73. The Cybersecurity Information Sharing Act became law in 2015. Which of the following is least likely established by the Cybersecurity Information Sharing Act?
A. There will be a reduction in privacy violations (correct)
B. There will be an improvement in cybersecurity
C. There will be an improvement in privacy
D. There will be a reduction in security incidents
Explanation:
The Cybersecurity Information Sharing Act is about security, not privacy. Although security and privacy are connected and an improvement in security is likely an improvement in privacy (option C), complying with the Cybersecurity Information Sharing will not likely lead, at least not directly, to a reduction in privacy violations.

74. You request your personal information from the U.S. government, as allowed by a relevant law. Which law provides private right of action in case your personal information request is incorrectly denied?
A. The General Data Protection Regulation
B. The Judicial Redress Act (correct)
C. The Children's Online Privacy Protection Act
D. The USA PATRIOT Act
Explanation:
In principle the General Data Protection Regulation could be correct, but it is more likely that the answer here is the Judicial Redress Act of 2015, which provides private right of action in case you request your personal information from the U.S. government and this is denied without a valid reason.

75. Court records are often published online. Which of the following personal information is least likely taken out before publishing court records?
A. A young offender's personal information
B. The debts of the accused
C. The websites visited by the offender (correct)
D. Details of the illness of the offender
Explanation:
Of the options provided, the websites the offender visited are the least privacy-sensitive and likely relevant to the court case.

76. Data retention programs are important and can help e-discovery. Which of the following is the least important part of a data retention program?
A. Determining the storage medium (correct)
B. Determining which documents/files to include
C. Determining the retention period
D. Taking into account the Sedona Conference guidelines
Explanation:
Data retention programs should pertain to which (type of) data needs to be deleted, and when the data should be deleted. The storage medium is irrelevant (whether you store something on a USB stick or a server likely does not influence how long you are allowed to keep the data). The Sedona conference guidelines concern e-discovery compliance through data retention policies, and are therefore relevant.

77. There are a number of federal privacy laws in the U.S. which provide privacy protection. Which of the following was the first national privacy law?
A. The Fair and Accurate Credit Transactions Act
B. The Children's Online Privacy Protection Act
C. The Controlling the Assault of Non-Solicited Pornography And Marketing Act
D. The Fair Credit Reporting Act (correct)
Explanation:
This is perhaps a useless fact to know, but there will be questions like this on the exam so you will have to be prepared. Do not focus too much on useless facts, you do not need to have a perfect score. Also, some questions are not counted towards your score, meaning some questions can be left unanswered without any consequences.

78. In the U.S., employees are generally employed under employment at will. Which of the following can provide the greatest privacy protection for an employee?
A. Health and safety requirements
B. State law
C. Non-discrimination laws
D. A contract (correct)
Explanation:
All mentioned options provide privacy protection. In a contract, however, you are free to include many binding aspects that can improve privacy, and option D is therefore the correct answer.

79. Which of the following is least likely a privacy risk of a bring your own device policy?
A. The company accidentally collects sensitive personal information it is not allowed to collect
B. Unauthorized access of personal information on the company network after opening a malicious email attachment (correct)
C. Company data floats around on personal devices, regardless of the data's classification
D. If a company is obliged to comply with a request to delete personal information, it can become overly complicated
Explanation:
The risk of opening a malicious attachment is likely the same regardless of whether an employee uses a company device or his/her own device. Here you will have to assume that the bring your own device policy specifies a level of virus protection or that there are other security measures in place.

80. An organization is looking to hire a Greek-speaking employee and takes out an advertisement in a newspaper in Greece. Which of the following background screening level is the maximum allowed for a remote office job?
A. Level 1 – conduct a job interview (correct)
B. Level 2 – conduct a psychometric test
C. Level 3 – conduct a polygraph test
D. Level 4 – require a blood sample
Explanation:
A Greek resident is targeted, who will even work in Greece (remotely). The General Data Protection Regulation therefore applies (Greece is a member of the European Union). Assuming it is a job only important for Greek language skills, a psychometric test would result in the collection of personal information that is not necessary for evaluating the suitability for the job. This means there is likely no legal basis for level 2, meaning level 1 is the highest level allowed. This reasoning also works when applying the Fair Information Practice Principles.

81. The Investigative Consumer Reporting Agency Act is stricter than the Fair Credit Reporting Act as regards investigative consumer reports. Which of the following is not required to be disclosed under the Investigative Consumer Reporting Agency Act?
A. The telephone number of the investigative consumer reporting agency
B. The fact that a report may be obtained
C. The email address of the investigative consumer report agency (correct)
D. What the permissible purpose of the report is
Explanation:
An email address is not required. A phone number is required though.

82. Video surveillance can be quite invasive. Which of the following is a way for video surveillance to fall outside the scope of federal records and stored-record statutes?
A. If the unions agree to the surveillance
B. If an employer uses closed-circuit television without sound (correct)
C. If the employer performs a privacy risk assessment prior to commencing surveillance
D. If the employer has not employed staff based on a contract
Explanation:
If no sound is recorded, CCTV falls outside the scope of the federal records and stored-records statutes. This makes sense, considering employers cannot listen in on conversations if no sound is recorded.

Use this case for the next two questions:
Allergens have become of increasing importance with the growing population since companies will try to widen their customer base and virtue signal how well they take care of their customers' needs. This has led to companies weighing revenue against inclusiveness.

A company producing artisanal cookies has decided to explore whether it would lose or gain customers if it changed its recipes to take into account allergies, and specifically which allergies it would have to take into account to become most profitable. The option of an extra product line with solely allergen-free cookies was also on the table, although this would entail setting up a new production facility so the different product lines cannot contaminate the allergen-free cookies.

The company has no idea how to approach the situation. At first, a survey was placed on the company's website. However, this came back with mostly useless responses, since the company's existing customers were obviously not allergic to any of the current ingredients. Then, the company approached a social media company. The social media company had access to the profiles it created for its users, including any allergens, which it derived from the content posted, shared, and liked by the user. According to the social media company, the information they provided has a 95% accuracy rate.

No personal information was sent to the artisanal cookie company, only an overview of the allergens and the percentage of users of the social media company that likely was allergic to these allergens was provided. In addition, the information was further divided into which customers were likely to buy cookies, and which were likely to pay extra for artisanal cookies. Lastly, the geographical distribution was provided, so it can be seen where the allergens have the biggest negative impact.

83. The social media company knows it has valuable and sensitive personal information and has created procedures with security practices. What are these procedures?
A. Technical security
B. Physical security
C. Organizational security
D. Administrative security (correct)
Explanation:
A procedure is administrative security. The measures described in the procedure can be of the other categories, but the procedure itself is administrative security.

84. Which of the following is true regarding the disclosure when the cookie company calls a recent new customer, considering the Telemarketing Sales Rule?
A. If the intent is to evaluate customer satisfaction and potentially sell more, disclosure is not required
B. Even if no sales are intended to be made, disclosure is required
C. Disclosure is always required, especially if there is a prior business relationship
D. If sales are potentially going to be made, disclosure needs to happen at the beginning of the call (correct)
Explanation:
When a telemarketer has the intention of selling, this needs to be disclosed at the beginning of the call.

85. Which of the following best describes how state law is created?
A. The governor passes the bill, and the state legislature signs it into law
B. The state legislature passes the bill, and the governor signs it into law (correct)
C. The state attorney general passes the bill, and the governor signs it into law
D. The state legislature passes the bill, and the state attorney general signs it into law
Explanation:
Option B is the correct answer. Remember all actors in the law-making process and their role. At the state level, it is the governor instead of the president that signs bills into law.

86. Which state law explicitly excludes web hosting services?
A. The Delaware Online Privacy and Protection Act (correct)
B. The California Privacy Rights Act
C. Washington Biometric Privacy law HB 1493
D. Nevada SB 538
Explanation:
The Delaware Online Privacy and Protection Act excludes web hosting services that have nothing to do with creating/maintaining the actual website.

87. Which of the following is not required by the Delaware Online Privacy and Protection Act?
A. Websites must have a process for informing users of changes in the privacy policy
B. Websites are not allowed to advertise tanning beds to anyone younger than 18 years
C. Websites are forbidden to track users (correct)
D. Users can request changes to their personal information
Explanation:
Websites can track users, but they need to inform them of the tracking. So, they only need to inform.

88. The California Consumer Privacy Act grants consumers certain rights. Which of the following is not a likely result of the rights granted under the California Consumer Privacy Act?
A. The consumer cannot be subject to higher prices after opting out of his/her personal information being sold
B. The consumer can request a copy of his/her personal information free of charge
C. The consumer can pursue private civil action
D. The consumer can forbid personal information is sent to third parties (correct)
Explanation:
You cannot completely forbid personal information from being sent to third parties. Think of an address needing to be sent to the postal service in order to deliver the product you ordered. Laws will therefore at most restrict personal information being sent to third parties, but not forbid it.

89. Which of the following is required under the California Electronic Communications and Privacy Act?
A. The Fourth Amendment of the U.S. Constitution provides roughly similar protection
B. It pertains to all personal information of Californians
C. It pertains to all personal information stored in California
D. Law enforcement officials need a warrant to search a Californian's web browsing history (correct)
Explanation:
All options have something missing and are incomplete or incorrect. Option D is correct, as the California Electronic Communications and Privacy Act requires a warrant to search Californians' web browsing history. It also includes other electronic information, such as text messages and information about how/when you communicated with someone.

90. Which of the following is most likely going to reduce the risk of non-compliance with state privacy law?
A. Identify and delete all assigned unique identifiers to the organization's customers
B. Ensure customer bank account numbers are deleted after a transaction has been completed
C. Hiring a privacy officer
D. Identify and delete all social security numbers the organization has collected (correct)
Explanation:
Social security numbers are one of the most sensitive types of personal information. It makes sense that deleting them reduces the risk of non-compliance significantly. You should be able to reason this way without necessarily knowing which state laws apply.

Exam 2:

1. Consent decrees can avoid admission of guilt. Which of the following enters into a consent decree?
A. The judicial branch
B. The legislative branch
C. The executive branch
D. The Federal Communications Commission

2. In Connecticut, what would "any person who conducts business in this state, and who, in the ordinary course of such person's business, owns, licenses, or maintains computerized data that includes personal information" be?
A. A data controller
B. A business associate
C. A data subject
D. A covered entity

3. The powers of the executive branch are mentioned specifically in which of the following?
A. Article II of the U.S. Constitution
B. The Federal Trade Commission handbook
C. The relevant legislation regarding unfair and deceptive practices
D. The Controlling the Assault of Non-Solicited Pornography And Marketing Act

4. Which of the following is least likely influenced by a precedent?
A. Case law
B. Common law
C. A jury of your peers
D. Stare decisis

5. Which of the following fits the concept of preemption least?
A. The Health Insurance Portability and Accountability Act
B. State law being stricter than federal law
C. State law being less strict than federal law
D. The Children's Online Privacy Protection Act

6. Which of the following is true regarding changes to the U.S. Constitution?
A. The U.S. Constitution can be changed, only by the president
B. If the people vote for change through a nationwide referendum, the U.S. Constitution must be changed
C. The U.S. Constitution cannot legally be changed
D. Article V allows for changes, although this has never occurred

7. Which of the following signs proposed bills into state law?
A. The legislative branch
B. The judicial branch
C. The president
D. The governor

8. A contract contains details regarding what the signing parties agree to. What is the trade-off by the recipient of the goods or services called?
A. Collateral
B. Tender
C. Consideration
D. Exchange

9. In case an organization breaks the law and violates your privacy, you might want to sue. What should be included in that law?
A. Private right of action
B. A responsibility article
C. The need for a contract
D. It should be an executive order

10. Which of the following is least likely true regarding common law?
A. Common law may override aspects of constitutional law
B. Common law can be traced back to the English court system
C. Common law is based on principles never included in legislation
D. Common law cannot exist without case law

11. Which of the following is most likely false regarding contracts?
A. A breach of contract is a dispute between two parties
B. A business associate agreement is a contract
C. A privacy notice posted on a website and read by the user before sharing personal information is a contract
D. Violations of a contract can result in the involvement of law enforcement to resolve the breach

12. If the California Consumer Privacy Act contains private right of action, which of the following is most likely true?
A. You can sue an online shop that collected too much personal information
B. You can request the Federal Trade Commission to enter into a settlement for you
C. All parties, including the aggrieved, can bring legal action
D. You can sue a university if it mishandled your personal information leading to a breach

13. Which of the following is least likely true in a tort case?
A. A contract has been breached
B. One party has committed a tortuous act
C. The tort case involves civil litigation
D. There has been negligence or an invasion of privacy

14. Anonymization is similar to de-identification. Which of the following laws will most likely result in the requirement for the anonymization of personal information?
A. The Fair and Accurate Credit Transactions Act
B. The General Data Protection Regulation
C. The Controlling the Assault of Non-Solicited Pornography And Marketing Act
D. The Health Insurance Portability and Accountability Act

Use this case for the next two questions:
An organic farm in Oregon called *Oreganic farming* has recently decided to start selling raw milk. Although one of the consumers of raw milk recently died after drinking raw milk elsewhere in the U.S., business is rapidly growing for the farm.

The farm started to see the need to approach things professionally, as well as the need to engage in extra activities to receive federal subsidies. One of these extra activities is an apprenticeship program, consisting of both on-the-job learning, assignments, and a quarterly exam. The program is a great success, as there is an economic crisis and apprentices are getting paid.

In order to move with the times, the farm has set up an online shop. The shop sells all products produced by the farm that can be sold with a higher profit margin than if the products were sold to a bigger re-seller. Raw milk, however, cannot be purchased online. In order to purchase raw milk, an appointment needs to be made for a specific time to pick up the milk, so that freshness can be guaranteed. The appointments are also made online.

To show off the success of the apprentice program, the farm has dedicated a section of its website to information about the current apprentices. This includes photos, email addresses, the phase of the apprenticeship, and personal testimonies. The apprentices had no choice regarding whether the information was placed on the website, except that the testimony was provided voluntarily.

The farm also hired an on-site veterinarian. Coincidentally the veterinarian has completed an associate degree in nursing and is therefore qualified to treat the apprentices for minor injuries. Due to this service's convenience, the apprentices make frequent use of the veterinarian's services.

15. The company enters into a consent decree. For how many years is the consent decree enforced?
A. 5 years
B. 50 years
C. 10 years
D. 20 years

16. What is likely a valid privacy consideration for the medical services provided to the apprentices?
A. Provide the treatment free of charge so that the Health Insurance Portability and Accountability Act does not apply
B. Take into account Occupational Safety and Health Act requirements regarding the need for the medical services
C. Avoid apprentices bringing their private pets to the veterinarian
D. Cut off treatment after the apprenticeship

17. The farm posts certain elements of its apprentices online. What can this be called in case the Family Educational Rights and Privacy Act applies?
A. Student information
B. Apprentice directory
C. Directory information
D. Personal data

18. Laws regarding personal information are referred to in different ways. Which of the following is the least common way to refer to such a law in the U.S.?
A. Data protection law
B. Privacy law
C. Data privacy law
D. Information privacy law

19. Security at airports can be quite invasive. Which type of privacy concerns the physical security checks?
A. Territorial privacy
B. Bodily privacy
C. Communications privacy
D. Information privacy

20. Which of the following is not a Fair Information Practice Principle?
A. A collector's legitimate interest
B. Use and retention
C. The quality of the personal information
D. A person's access to his/her personal information

21. The General Data Protection Regulation contains the role of a data processor. Which of the following is least likely a data processor?
A. Business associates
B. An organization's payroll department
C. A freelance employee hired by a larger organization
D. A party subject to a data processing agreement

22. Which of the following best describes the difference between a data flow map and a data inventory?
A. Data flow maps are mandatory only in U.S. organizations, data inventories are not
B. Data flow maps are part of the data inventory
C. A data inventory is required for internationally operating organizations, whereas a data flow map supports the data inventory
D. The data inventory is an element of the data flow map

23. Obtaining consent before collecting personal information can be tricky. Which of the following is not true regarding consent in the European Union?
A. It needs to be given by an informed person
B. The consent needs to be freely given
C. It can only be for a specific process
D. The consent is fully reversible at all times

24. A company in the European Union is using a third party for certain services involving personal information. Which of the following is not necessary for the third party in order to qualify as a data processor?
A. A data processing agreement is in place
B. The third party cannot determine the means and purposes of the processing of the personal information
C. The third party has a legal basis for processing the personal information
D. The third party has access to the personal information

25. Which of the following is a risk when appointing a data protection officer instead of a privacy officer for an organizational branch in the European Union?
A. The data protection officer not being aware of the U.S. privacy regulation and the purposes the organization uses the personal information for
B. That the data protection officer cannot be fired when giving advice against management's will
C. The data protection officer advising to update the data inventory
D. The data protection officer disagreeing with the privacy officers in other countries

26. Which of the following will most likely be considered a data controller in the European Union?
A. A cloud server storing personal information
B. A third party receiving a data transfer at their request
C. An external payroll service
D. Software as a service provider human resource management software

27. Which of the following is most likely false regarding the Fair Information Practice Principles?
A. Compliance with the Fair Information Practice Principles is not a requirement of the Family Educational Rights and Privacy Act
B. The Asia-Pacific Economic Cooperation principles are similar to the Fair Information Practice Principles
C. Compliance with the Fair Information Practice Principles results in compliance with the General Data Protection Regulation
D. The Protection of Personal Information Act contains several Fair Information Practice Principles

28. Of the following, what is the best moment to provide the possibility to opt out?
A. At the beginning of a data entry process
B. When sending an email
C. Before clicking 'submit' on an online form
D. When setting up a new device

29. Which of the following is not a valid way of transferring personal information from the European Union to the U.S.?
A. Binding Corporate Rules
B. EU-US Privacy Shield or its replacement
C. User consent
D. A transfer agreement

Use this case for the next two questions:
An ad block company provides a browser plugin that prevents advertisements from showing while browsing the internet. It works great, for most websites, but some websites detect that an ad blocker is being used and block the content of the website to display properly.

The ad block company provides the browser plugin for free since people have been getting used to receiving software for free. In return, they require the user to consent to letting the company monitor the user's internet activity, as well as the user's location (based on the IP address). This has proven tremendously profitable since many advertisers start realizing that tracking cookies are not going to work for the more tech-savvy consumers.

A database of users is stored securely on the company's servers, with the employees having access to the information on a need-to-know basis. Not even the CEO has access to all data in the company, despite being the highest level of management. This is much to the dismay of the CEO, but the CEO does realize it is best for the company and respects (and approved) the policies drafted by the Chief Information Security Officer.

The browser plugin is activated the moment the user starts up the internet browser. Ironically, the user needs to consent to receiving marketing emails from the ad block software company. Most users gladly trade a more pleasant internet experience for a few easily ignorable emails. The list of email addresses used for the targeted marketing, as well as the profiles created of each user based on browsing habits, is protected with a password. Without the password it is just a set of data that appears random.

30. The ad block software company entered into a consent decree for certain practices but customers claim the company fails to comply with the consent decree. What will likely happen?
A. The Federal Trade Commission issues a fine
B. The Federal Trade Commission goes to court
C. The Federal Trade Commission starts an investigation
D. The Federal Trade Commission provides a second chance for compliance with the consent decree

31. There is a contract between the ad block software company and the customer. What does this contract have to contain?
A. Consideration, acceptance, offer
B. Offer, terms, value-added
C. Value-added, signature, offer
D. Offer, counteroffer, acceptance

32. Which of the following is true regarding adequacy decisions in the European Union?
A. The adequacy decisions are issued by the data protection authority
B. An adequacy decision results in not needing data processing agreements anymore
C. Only the data controllers in the country are affected by the adequacy decision
D. Countries can be deemed partly adequate

33. Regarding privacy in Canada, which of the following is false?
A. Consent is a valid basis for using personal information
B. Canada is deemed partially adequate
C. The government works under a different privacy law than the private sector
D. The private sector law is the Protection of Personal Information Act

34. Which of the following is least likely a data breach when processing the personal information of citizens of the European Union?
A. Stolen personal information
B. Lost personal information
C. Illegally processed personal information
D. A wrongfully addressed email containing personal information

35. Which of the following is least likely true regarding privacy programs?
A. Privacy programs result in increased awareness
B. Privacy programs are required under the General Data Protection Regulation
C. Privacy programs are sponsored by the CEO
D. The number of privacy incidents will increase

36. Which of the following is most important if you have an international vendor processing personal information for your organization?
A. To determine whether a data processing agreement is required
B. To ensure audit rights
C. To designate personal information for processing within the state only
D. To ensure the bidding process abides by the rules

37. An organization fails to meet the requirements for data collection from children. Which entity is most likely going to take action?
A. The Federal Communications Commission
B. The Federal Trade Commission
C. The Department of Justice
D. The attorney general

38. The Children's Online Privacy Protection Act has improved online privacy for children. Which of the following is not required by the Children's Online Privacy Protection Act when using the personal information of children?
A. Express consent
B. Affirmation
C. Opt-in
D. Op-out

39. The Federal Trade Commission was notified of a major unfair practice but is unable to investigate. Which of the following is most likely the case?
A. The Federal Trade Commission does not investigate unfair practices
B. It concerns a deceptive practice instead
C. It concerns a nonprofit organization
D. It concerns a multinational organization

40. At some point, an order issued by the Federal Trade Commission becomes final. After how many days will this be?
A. 90 days
B. 30 days
C. 60 days
D. 365 days

41. Which of the following is false regarding consent decrees?
A. A company does not admit guilt
B. Can lead to enforcement in federal court
C. Consent decrees are the Federal Trade Commission's sole means of enforcement
D. Consent decrees can apply for up to twenty years

42. Which of the following is the best example of an unfair trade practice?
A. Making false claims in a privacy notice
B. Leaving out information in a privacy statement
C. Sharing information with a foreign third party
D. Not implementing adequate security measures

43. Which of the following is not a requirement for de-identification under the Health Insurance Portability and Accountability Act privacy rule?
A. Encryption of 256-bit when used for medical research
B. Removing at least 18 data elements
C. Having a certified small risk of re-identification
D. Having a reasonable basis to believe the individuals cannot be identified

44. During an investigation you find out a list of passwords was accessed by a third party. Which of the following reduces the potential damage done in such an instance the least?
A. If the data was hashed
B. If the data was salted
C. If the data was encrypted
D. If the data was compressed

45. What was an initial goal of the Health Insurance Portability and Accountability Act?
A. Improving the quality of healthcare delivery
B. Improving the efficiency of healthcare delivery
C. Improving medical privacy practices
D. Improving the security during the handling of medical data

Use this case for the next four questions:
Nowadays everything is being recorded all the time. Every car has a dashboard camera, and every cyclist is wearing a camera. One way to wear a camera is on a helmet. Helm-cam is a company that produces the most popular type of helmet camera. From cyclist helmets to motorcycle helmets, the company produces all types.

The cameras can work by simply inserting a micro-SD card into the device. This is inconvenient since the video will have to be copied from the micro-SD card, meaning the micro-SD card needs to be removed from the camera and inserted into a different device. Many users have complained about this inconvenience.

After having listened to its customers' complaints, Helm-cam decided to add two more options to get the video to a different device. The first method works via Bluetooth only. If a user selects this option, the video from the camera will be captured on the phone of the user. This requires less processing power from the camera, improving battery life. The second option involves a Bluetooth connection with the user's phone as well, but instead of storing the video on the user's phone, the video is stored directly in the cloud. The company figured it can charge an extra monthly fee for the use of the cloud space.

Since the company now processes a lot more personal information, namely the videos stored on the cloud, it hires a privacy officer. The privacy officer is put to work right away, as the data breach occurs on his first day. This eventually leads to a court case, as protection proved to be inadequate and customers were informed of the breach too late.

46. You purchased a helmet camera, and it suddenly gives you the option to either render the device useless or accept an invasive new privacy policy. Which entity is most likely going to seek compensation?
A. The Federal Trade Commission
B. The Federal Communications Commission
C. The Department of Justice
D. The state attorney

47. During the court case, the judge says the case is similar to another case and copies the decision. What is likely the case?
A. Mens rea
B. Stare decisis
C. Common law
D. Decisis trancendus

48. The company incorrectly claims not to collect location data. Which of the following does this likely constitute?
A. A deceptive trade practice
B. An unfair trade practice
C. The violation of a consent decree
D. A violation of the acceptance of the contract in the form of the privacy notice

49. Your cloud-stored videos have been accessed by an outsider. This happened because you opened a malicious file. Which of the following tort is most likely applicable?
A. Intrusion upon seclusion
B. Trespass to land
C. Invasion of solitude
D. Intentional infliction of emotional distress

50. Covered entities are defined in the Transaction Rule, the Privacy Rule, and the Security Rule. In which of these three is the definition of covered entities most strict?
A. The Transaction Rule
B. The Privacy Rule
C. The Security Rule
D. All are equally strict

51. Which of the following is least likely covered by the 'Confidentiality of Substance Use Disorder Patient Records Rule'?
A. A free psychologist partially specialized in addiction
B. A doctor in a public hospital, specialized in damage to the liver caused by alcohol
C. A substance abuse counselor in a government hospital
D. A person's general practitioner, discussing the issues

52. A data inventory can help organizations see which personal information it uses. Which of the following requires a data inventory?
A. The Children's Online Privacy Protection Act
B. The Gramm-Leach-Bliley Act
C. The California Online Privacy Protection Act
D. The Fair Credit Reporting Act

53. Which of the following contributed the least to the need for the Fair Credit Reporting Act?
A. The increasingly competitive labor market
B. The increasing importance of consumer credit
C. The increase in inaccurate information
D. The consequences of inaccurate information

54. What is the primary use of consumer reports?
A. Assisting in assessing eligibility for credit
B. Assisting in the recruitment process
C. Assisting law enforcement agencies
D. Evaluation for opening a bank account

55. In case a company fails to properly investigate consumers who attempt to dispute the information in their consumer reports, which of the following is most likely to bring enforcement action?
A. The Consumer Financial Protection Bureau
B. The Federal Trade Commission
C. State attorneys general
D. The Federal Communications Commission

56. The Gramm-Leach-Bliley Act privacy rule places requirements on financial institutions. Which of the following is such a requirement?
A. Opting out of joint marketing efforts with third parties
B. Refrain from disclosing personal information to third parties
C. Opting out of having non-public personal information shared with non-affiliated third parties
D. Provide a monthly update on changes in the privacy notice

57. The parents of a student who is 21 are able to request the student's education records, much to the student's dismay. Which of the following is most likely the case?
A. The student is a dependent for tax purposes
B. It concerns a foreign exchange student
C. The student is no longer attending the educational institution
D. The student has consented

58. Which of the following is not a right provided to students by the Family Educational Rights and Privacy Act?
A. To review and amend their education records
B. To receive an annual notice of their rights
C. To control disclosure of education records to others
D. To file a complaint

59. The Family Educational Rights and Privacy Act has several criteria for consent. Which of the following is not one of the criteria for consent?
A. Records subject to disclosure must be specific
B. The consent must be dated
C. The right to withdraw consent must be specified
D. The consent cannot be verbal

60. The 'K-12 School Service Provider Pledge to Safeguard Privacy' is which of the following?
A. Sectoral law
B. Federal law
C. Self-regulation
D. State law

61. The way we consume video entertainment has radically changed over the years, and moved to mostly streaming services. Which of the following is not applicable to streaming services?
A. None of the options
B. The General Data Protection Regulation
C. The Video Privacy Protection Act
D. The Cable Communications Policy Act

62. Opt-outs are frequently used. In which situation is an opt-out least likely allowed?
A. A 'please call me' button
B. An 'I do not wish to receive emails' button
C. A 'contact me' box
D. A preferred method of contact box

Use this case for the next three questions:
An employer in California employs 700 employees. For some levels in the organization it is employment at will, for other groups an employment contract is signed by the employee and the employer. The remuneration the employer offers is quite competitive, and employees are happy to work there, with or without an employment contract.

The company is keen on collecting data on its employees for efficiency improvement analysis. This resulted in data lakes of which less than 5% is actually used in efficiency improvement efforts. Despite having been told that having the data without needing to have it poses a risk to the organization, the CEO does not want to discard the data because 'it might be of use someday'. CCTV images are part of the data collected by the employer. Advanced facial recognition is used to detect which employee is in the image. The software is not advanced enough yet to identify the tasks or actions the employees in the images are performing, but slowly the software is being improved towards that end.

Unions are meddling when it comes to labor conditions. Whenever an improvement for union members can be arranged, the unions are quick to force negotiations with the employer. Up until now, the unions were not aware of the invasiveness of the data-collecting practices of the employer, but at the moment a data analyst is growing a conscience and is preparing to inform the unions of the employer's invasive practices.

63. There is a contract between the company and the employee. What would the job description and the salary be referred to as?
A. Terms
B. Bargain
C. Acceptance
D. Consideration

64. The employer scans the emails of its employees. Which type of privacy does this have the biggest impact on?
A. Bodily privacy
B. Territorial privacy
C. Geographic privacy
D. Information privacy

65. The employees accuse the employer of excessive video monitoring. Excessive video monitoring is most likely a violation of which class of privacy?
A. Bodily privacy
B. Territorial privacy
C. Information privacy
D. Communications privacy

66. Which of the following cannot access the National Do Not Call Registry?
A. Sellers
B. Consumers
C. Telemarketers
D. Service providers of sellers/telemarketers

67. Federal Rule of Civil Procedure 45 contains requirements for subpoenas. Which of the following is not a requirement for a subpoena?
A. A subpoena must be served electronically
B. A subpoena must contain the civil action number
C. A subpoena must contain the title of the action
D. The person's right to seek modification of the subpoena must be included

68. Which of the following is least likely an exception to attorney-client privilege?
A. The information is pertinent to the case, but the client does not agree to share it
B. The information will incriminate the client but can save someone's life
C. The information will not incriminate the client and can save someone's life
D. The client agrees to share the information, regardless of it being pertinent to the case

69. Which of the following is least likely true regarding the Electronic Communications Privacy Act and similar laws?
A. Interception is allowed if one of the parties agrees to it in the U.S.
B. The Electronic Communications Privacy Act resulted in emails falling under the ban on interception
C. Anything over a wire, when privacy can reasonably be expected, is covered
D. An exception is when the interception is done in any ordinary course of business

70. How can you best describe a discovery request?
A. E-discovery in a criminal case
B. A request from a party in a lawsuit
C. An order by a judge to release information pertinent to the case
D. Similar to a national security letter

71. During litigation, a protective order can be sought. Which of the following best describes a protective order?
A. The removal of a name
B. A whistle-blower procedure
C. Privilege granted, such as spousal privilege
D. Information for an attorney's eyes only

72. Workplace privacy can be tricky. Which of the following is least likely true regarding workplace privacy?
A. The General Data Protection Regulation can be applicable in the U.S. workplace
B. Employers have an incentive to collect a lot of personal information on their (prospective) employees
C. There are laws that require the collection of personal information before hiring an employee
D. The European Union has more laws providing employee privacy than the U.S.

73. In the U.S., employees are generally employed using employment at will. Which of the following can provide the greatest privacy protection?
A. The General Data Protection Regulation
B. Collective bargaining agreements
C. Local state law
D. Background check laws

74. The Department of Labor administers several laws. Which of the following is not administered by the Department of Labor?
A. The Age Discrimination in Employment Act
B. The Occupational Safety and Health Act
C. The Fair Labor Standards Act
D. The Employee Retirement Income Security Act

75. Employers often overstep privacy boundaries. Which of the following is least likely forbidden at an office?
A. Closed-circuit television in the locker room
B. Closed-circuit television in the restroom
C. Opening an employee's personal mail
D. Listening in on personal phone conversations

76. Which of the following is most likely true for HR-related privacy issues?
A. HR-related privacy issues are overshadowed by consumer privacy risks for traditional organizations
B. Employment at will reduces the risk of HR-related privacy issues
C. The introduction of IT resulted in HR-related privacy issues requiring attention
D. HR-related privacy issues form a risk to all organizations

77. In the U.S. several laws forbid discrimination in employment. Which of the following could be a valid reason to discriminate?
A. Consent of the candidate or employee regarding the use of the personal information on the basis of which discrimination takes place
B. Discrimination based on pregnancy revealed after a voluntary drug test
C. An employer found out through a mutual acquaintance that an employee handling finances has filed for bankruptcy
D. Not hiring a disabled person for manual work

78. During employment, employers cannot use lie detectors. Which of the following is not an example of a lie detector?
A. Email analyses
B. Polygraphs
C. Voice stress analyzers
D. Psychological stress evaluators

79. Data loss prevention can be of great value when trying to detect when employees sneak out sensitive data. Which of the following is not an element of a successful data loss prevention program?
A. Data governance
B. Data discovery
C. Training and awareness
D. A legal basis

Use this case for the next three questions:
Fair trade coffee is increasing in popularity due to the growing awareness amongst consumers of the consequences of unfair trade. Not only has this led to the bigger coffee producers increasing fairness in their supply chain and using that as a selling point in their advertisement, but farms in coffee-producing countries also started selling their coffee online through coffee traders.

One coffee trader allows consumers to order coffee from the farmer of their choosing, using the coffee trader as a middleman. The coffee trader even placed photos and profiles of the local farmers on its website, including a live video feed if the farmers has put up cameras on his coffee plantation.

After ordering through the coffee trader, something called a 'flavor preference profile' is created, and the consumer is informed regularly by email about harvests that fit the customer's flavor preference profile. There is no possibility of opting out, which customers do not seem to mind.

On top of the regular emailing, the coffee trader attempts to reach its larger customers by phone from time to time in order to secure larger sales. Although some of these larger customers are individuals, they order suspiciously large amounts of coffee, which the coffee trader chooses to ignore. The coffee trader even receives large cash payments from time to time, which does not seem to worry the coffee trader.

80. The coffee trader extends credit to some of its customers but does not use consumer reports. Which of the following is most likely true for the coffee trader?
A. The coffee trader will need to implement a red flag program
B. The personal information processed will have to comply with stricter requirements
C. The personal information processed will fall within the scope of the General Data Protection Regulation
D. Consumers will have the same access rights to the personal information used as with consumer reports

81. An affiliate of the coffee trader can transfer personal information from the EU under an adequacy decision, but the government cannot. In which country is the affiliate located?
A. Canada
B. Israel
C. New Zealand
D. Japan

82. The trader calls customers who placed themselves on the National Do Not Call Registry. How long ago can these customers have made their previous purchase?
A. Maximum 16 months ago
B. Maximum 20 months ago
C. Maximum 18 months ago
D. Maximum 12 months ago

83. Which of the following is true regarding federal versus state privacy laws?
A. State law generally preempts federal law
B. Federal law never preempts state law
C. State laws specify whether federal law preempts it
D. Federal law generally preempts state law

84. Which law amends the California Consumer Privacy Act?
A. The California FTC Act
B. The California Privacy Amendment Act
C. The California Privacy Rights Act
D. The Federal Communications Committee California rules of procedure

85. Which of the following is not true under Nevada SB 538?
A. All websites in Nevada are required to post a privacy policy
B. The privacy policy needs to contain the effective date
C. The privacy policy needs to contain a process for correcting personally identifiable information
D. Web hosting services are excluded from liabilities for violations

86. The California Privacy Rights Act grants consumers certain rights. Which of the following is such a right granted under the California Privacy Rights Act?
A. The right to opt out
B. The right to correction
C. The right to know
D. The right to access

87. Under the California Consumer Privacy Act, it can be requested to delete certain personal information. If a company refuses to delete your personal information, which of the following is least likely the case?
A. The company has a contract with a third party involving the personal information
B. The company has to complete a transaction requiring your personal information
C. The company is investigating fraud and your personal information is crucial to the investigation
D. For tax reporting requirements, your personal information needs to remain with the company for a certain period

88. Which of the following is most likely going to reduce the risk of non-compliance with state privacy law?
A. Hiring a privacy officer
B. Appointing a data protection officer
C. Applying role-based access control
D. Collecting only the personal information needed to conduct business

89. Under California's AB 1950, which of the following, in combination with a person's name, would least likely constitute a data breach if leaked?
A. Debit card number
B. Telephone number
C. Driver's license number
D. Automated license plate recognition information

90. States have enacted breach notification laws. Which state was the first to do so?
A. North Carolina
B. California
C. New York
D. Florida

Answer key exam 2:

1C, 2D, 3A, 4C, 5D, 6D, 7D, 8C, 9A, 10A, 11D, 12D, 13A, 14B, 15D, 16A, 17C, 18A, 19B, 20A, 21B, 22C, 23D, 24C, 25B, 26B, 27C, 28C, 29D, 30C, 31A, 32D, 33D, 34C, 35B, 36A, 37B, 38D, 39C, 40C, 41C, 42D, 43A, 44D, 45B, 46A, 47B, 48A, 49C, 50D, 51D, 52B, 53A, 54A, 55A, 56C, 57A, 58A, 59C, 60C, 61D, 62A, 63D, 64D, 65B, 66B, 67A, 68A, 69A, 70B, 71D, 72D, 73B, 74A, 75C, 76D, 77D, 78A, 79D, 80A, 81A, 82C, 83D, 84C, 85A, 86B, 87A, 88D, 89B, 90B

Correct answers and explanations for exam 2:

1. Consent decrees can avoid admission of guilt. Which of the following enters into a consent decree?
A. The judicial branch
B. The legislative branch
C. The executive branch (correct)
D. The Federal Communications Commission
Explanation:
The Federal Trade Commission is the party that an organization enters into a consent decree with. The Federal Trade Commission is part of the executive branch.

2. In Connecticut, what would "any person who conducts business in this state, and who, in the ordinary course of such person's business, owns, licenses, or maintains computerized data that includes personal information" be?
A. A data controller
B. A business associate
C. A data subject
D. A covered entity (correct)
Explanation:
See chapter 669 of the General Statutes of Connecticut. This is the definition of a covered entity.

3. The powers of the executive branch are mentioned specifically in which of the following?
A. Article II of the U.S. Constitution (correct)
B. The Federal Trade Commission handbook
C. The relevant legislation regarding unfair and deceptive practices
D. The Controlling the Assault of Non-Solicited Pornography And Marketing Act
Explanation:
Article II of the U.S. Constitution defines the powers of the executive branch. For the legislative branch, this is Article I and for the judicial branch, this is Article III.

4. Which of the following is least likely influenced by a precedent?
A. Case law
B. Common law
C. A jury of your peers (correct)
D. Stare decisis
Explanation:
The jury (of your peers) is solely tasked with determining whether someone is guilty, not, for example, with punishment. This is not influenced by previous verdicts.

5. Which of the following fits the concept of preemption least?
A. The Health Insurance Portability and Accountability Act
B. State law being stricter than federal law
C. State law being less strict than federal law
D. The Children's Online Privacy Protection Act (correct)
Explanation:
The Children's Online Privacy Protection Act preempts state law, but the Health Insurance Portability and Accountability Act does not. Options B and C miss the element of which law applies. Therefore, option D is the correct answer.

6. Which of the following is true regarding changes to the U.S. Constitution?
A. The U.S. Constitution can be changed, only by the president
B. If the people vote for change through a nationwide referendum, the U.S. Constitution must be changed
C. The U.S. Constitution cannot legally be changed
D. Article V allows for changes, although this has never occurred (correct)
Explanation:
Article V allows for changes if two-thirds of the state legislature wants a change.

7. Which of the following signs proposed bills into state law?
A. The legislative branch
B. The judicial branch
C. The president
D. The governor (correct)
Explanation:
The law-making process at the state level is similar to that at the federal level. However, the governor signs the proposed bills into law instead of the president.

8. A contract contains details regarding what the signing parties agree to. What is the trade-off by the recipient of the goods or services called?
A. Collateral
B. Tender
C. Consideration (correct)
D. Exchange
Explanation:
The trade-off is called consideration. The other elements are offer and acceptance.

9. In case an organization breaks the law and violates your privacy, you might want to sue. What should be included in that law?
A. Private right of action (correct)
B. A responsibility article
C. The need for a contract
D. It should be an executive order
Explanation:
As a person, you can only sue for the violation of a law (normally enforced by the government) if that law contains 'private right of action'.

10. Which of the following is least likely true regarding common law?
A. Common law may override aspects of constitutional law (correct)
B. Common law can be traced back to the English court system
C. Common law is based on principles never included in legislation
D. Common law cannot exist without case law
Explanation:
Constitutional law cannot be overridden. Common law principles are derived from previous jurisprudence, but cannot conflict with constitutional law.

11. Which of the following is most likely false regarding contracts?
A. A breach of contract is a dispute between two parties
B. A business associate agreement is a contract
C. A privacy notice posted on a website and read by the user before sharing personal information is a contract
D. Violations of a contract can result in the involvement of law enforcement to resolve the breach (correct)
Explanation:
Breaching a contract can result in a civil case, where one party tries to force the other party to uphold the contract or pay damages.

12. If the California Consumer Privacy Act contains private right of action, which of the following is most likely true?
A. You can sue an online shop that collected too much personal information
B. You can request the Federal Trade Commission to enter into a settlement for you
C. All parties, including the aggrieved, can bring legal action
D. You can sue a university if it mishandled your personal information leading to a breach (correct)
Explanation:
When a law contains private right of action, individuals can take action and this does not have to go through, for example, the Federal Trade Commission. Option C is incorrect because only the aggrieved can bring legal action. Option A might be correct, but it is not clear whether there are any adverse consequences due to the overcollection.

13. Which of the following is least likely true in a tort case?
A. A contract has been breached (correct)
B. One party has committed a tortuous act
C. The tort case involves civil litigation
D. There has been negligence or an invasion of privacy
Explanation:
Breach of contract likely pertains to contract law rather than tort law.

14. Anonymization is similar to de-identification. Which of the following laws will most likely result in the requirement for the anonymization of personal information?
A. The Fair and Accurate Credit Transactions Act
B. The General Data Protection Regulation (correct)
C. The Controlling the Assault of Non-Solicited Pornography And Marketing Act
D. The Health Insurance Portability and Accountability Act
Explanation:
The General Data Protection Regulation states its requirements no longer apply to 'personal data rendered anonymous in such a manner that the data subject is no longer identifiable.' The requirement here is 'no longer identifiable'. The Health Insurance Portability and Accountability Act has requirements for personal information used for research but does not require full anonymization. The phrasing of this question is intentionally vague and unclear, which is something you will find on the exam.

Use this case for the next two questions:
An organic farm in Oregon called *Oreganic farming* has recently decided to start selling raw milk. Although one of the consumers of raw milk recently died after drinking raw milk elsewhere in the U.S., business is rapidly growing for the farm.

The farm started to see the need to approach things professionally, as well as the need to engage in extra activities to receive federal subsidies. One of these extra activities is an apprenticeship program, consisting of both on-the-job learning, assignments, and a quarterly exam. The program is a great success, as there is an economic crisis and apprentices are getting paid.

In order to move with the times, the farm has set up an online shop. The shop sells all products produced by the farm that can be sold with a higher profit margin than if the products were sold to a bigger re-seller. Raw milk, however, cannot be purchased online. In order to purchase raw milk, an appointment needs to be made for a specific time to pick up the milk, so that freshness can be guaranteed. The appointments are also made online.

To show off the success of the apprentice program, the farm has dedicated a section of its website to information about the current apprentices. This includes photos, email addresses, the phase of the apprenticeship, and personal testimonies. The apprentices had no choice regarding whether the information was placed on the website, except that the testimony was provided voluntarily.

The farm also hired an on-site veterinarian. Coincidentally the veterinarian has completed an associate degree in nursing and is therefore qualified to treat the apprentices for minor injuries. Due to this service's convenience, the apprentices make frequent use of the veterinarian's services.

15. The company enters into a consent decree. For how many years is the consent decree enforced?
A. 5 years
B. 50 years
C. 10 years
D. 20 years (correct)
Explanation:
Consent decrees, and other administrative orders, are imposed for up to 20 years. This is established by the Sunset policy.

16. What is likely a valid privacy consideration for the medical services provided to the apprentices?
A. Provide the treatment free of charge so that the Health Insurance Portability and Accountability Act does not apply (correct)
B. Take into account Occupational Safety and Health Act requirements regarding the need for the medical services
C. Avoid apprentices bringing their private pets to the veterinarian
D. Cut off treatment after the apprenticeship
Explanation:
If there is no (electronic) payment, then the Health Insurance Portability and Accountability Act does not apply. The other options do not relate to privacy.

17. The farm posts certain elements of its apprentices online. What can this be called in case the Family Educational Rights and Privacy Act applies?
A. Student information
B. Apprentice directory
C. Directory information (correct)
D. Personal data
Explanation:
Since the farm receives federal funding, the Family Educational Rights and Privacy Act likely applies. Under the Family Educational Rights and Privacy Act, this information qualifies as directory information.

18. Laws regarding personal information are referred to in different ways. Which of the following is the least common way to refer to such a law in the U.S.?
A. Data protection law (correct)
B. Privacy law
C. Data privacy law
D. Information privacy law
Explanation:
Data protection law is more common in the European Union, as being incorporated in the General Data Protection Regulation. It is difficult to figure out what the logic is you are expected to apply, so flag the question to come back later if you do not see it right away.

19. Security at airports can be quite invasive. Which type of privacy concerns the physical security checks?
A. Territorial privacy
B. Bodily privacy (correct)
C. Communications privacy
D. Information privacy
Explanation:
Assuming the question concerns x-ray scans, pat downs, and cavity searches, this pertains to bodily privacy.

20. Which of the following is not a Fair Information Practice Principle?
A. A collector's legitimate interest (correct)
B. Use and retention
C. The quality of the personal information
D. A person's access to his/her personal information
Explanation:
A collector's legitimate interest, meaning why a collector would have a justified interest in collecting the personal information, is not part of the Fair Information Practice Principles.

21. The General Data Protection Regulation contains the role of a data processor. Which of the following is least likely a data processor?
A. Business associates
B. An organization's payroll department (correct)
C. A freelance employee hired by a larger organization
D. A party subject to a data processing agreement
Explanation:
A department, in this case the payroll department, is still part of the organization. It is therefore part of the organization that is the data controller. If the payroll would be outsourced to a third party, it would be a data processor. Since it is not, it is a data controller.

22. Which of the following best describes the difference between a data flow map and a data inventory?
A. Data flow maps are mandatory only in U.S. organizations, data inventories are not
B. Data flow maps are part of the data inventory
C. A data inventory is required for internationally operating organizations, whereas a data flow map supports the data inventory (correct)
D. The data inventory is an element of the data flow map
Explanation:
Data flow maps are generally not mandatory, they are generally not part of a data inventory and the data inventory is not an element of a data flow map. A data inventory is required under the General Data Protection Regulation for data controllers, and therefore likely required for internationally operating organizations (although you will have to assume the organization also operates in the European Union).

23. Obtaining consent before collecting personal information can be tricky. Which of the following is not true regarding consent in the European Union?
A. It needs to be given by an informed person
B. The consent needs to be freely given
C. It can only be for a specific process
D. The consent is fully reversible at all times (correct)
Explanation:
Although consent is required to be fully reversible at all times. Obviously, some things are permanent, like printing or broadcasting, hence it is practically not 100% reversible.

24. A company in the European Union is using a third party for certain services involving personal information. Which of the following is not necessary for the third party in order to qualify as a data processor?
A. A data processing agreement is in place
B. The third party cannot determine the means and purposes of the processing of the personal information
C. The third party has a legal basis for processing the personal information (correct)
D. The third party has access to the personal information
Explanation:
Only a data controller needs a legal basis for processing the personal information because the data controller determines the means and purposes. If the data processor does things to the personal information beyond the data controller's instructions, for that part the data processor becomes a data controller.

25. Which of the following is a risk when appointing a data protection officer instead of a privacy officer for an organizational branch in the European Union?
A. The data protection officer not being aware of the U.S. privacy regulation and the purposes the organization uses the personal information for
B. That the data protection officer cannot be fired when giving advice against management's will (correct)
C. The data protection officer advising to update the data inventory
D. The data protection officer disagreeing with the privacy officers in other countries
Explanation:
The position of a data protection officer is protected in the General Data Protection Regulation because the Data Protection Officer is required to be independent. So, the data protection officer cannot be fired for going against management's will by means of giving advice management does not agree with. This protection does not extend to privacy officers.

26. Which of the following will most likely be considered a data controller in the European Union?
A. A cloud server storing personal information
B. A third party receiving a data transfer at their request (correct)
C. An external payroll service
D. Software as a service provider human resource management software
Explanation:
If data is transferred at a third party's request, this means the third party must have a legal basis for processing it. This makes it a data controller.

27. Which of the following is most likely false regarding the Fair Information Practice Principles?
A. Compliance with the Fair Information Practice Principles is not a requirement of the Family Educational Rights and Privacy Act
B. The Asia-Pacific Economic Cooperation principles are similar to the Fair Information Practice Principles
C. Compliance with the Fair Information Practice Principles results in compliance with the General Data Protection Regulation (correct)
D. The Protection of Personal Information Act contains several Fair Information Practice Principles
Explanation:
Although the Fair Information Practice Principles are incorporated in the General Data Protection Regulation, there is more in the General Data Protection Regulation than just the Fair Information Practice Principles.

28. Of the following, what is the best moment to provide the possibility to opt out?
A. At the beginning of a data entry process
B. When sending an email
C. Before clicking 'submit' on an online form (correct)
D. When setting up a new device
Explanation:
Right before clicking submit is on time. If you provide the opt-out much earlier, the person might not yet have all the information to make the decision on whether or not to opt out. Option D is the second-best option, but is vague compared to option C.

29. Which of the following is not a valid way of transferring personal information from the European Union to the U.S.?
A. Binding Corporate Rules
B. EU-US Privacy Shield or its replacement
C. User consent
D. A transfer agreement (correct)
Explanation:
A transfer agreement, without any other measures, is not sufficient (unless the transfer agreement contains all elements of Binding Corporate Rules or model contracts). The other options are sufficient.

Use this case for the next two questions:
An ad block company provides a browser plugin that prevents advertisements from showing while browsing the internet. It works great, for most websites, but some websites detect that an ad blocker is being used and block the content of the website to display properly.

The ad block company provides the browser plugin for free since people have been getting used to receiving software for free. In return, they require the user to consent to letting the company monitor the user's internet activity, as well as the user's location (based on the IP address). This has proven tremendously profitable since many advertisers start realizing that tracking cookies are not going to work for the more tech-savvy consumers.

A database of users is stored securely on the company's servers, with the employees having access to the information on a need-to-know basis. Not even the CEO has access to all data in the company, despite being the highest level of management. This is much to the dismay of the CEO, but the CEO does realize it is best for the company and respects (and approved) the policies drafted by the Chief Information Security Officer.

The browser plugin is activated the moment the user starts up the internet browser. Ironically, the user needs to consent to receiving marketing emails from the ad block software company. Most users gladly trade a more pleasant internet experience for a few easily ignorable emails. The list of email addresses used for the targeted marketing, as well as the profiles created of each user based on browsing habits, is protected with a password. Without the password it is just a set of data that appears random.

30. The ad block software company entered into a consent decree for certain practices but customers claim the company fails to comply with the consent decree. What will likely happen?
A. The Federal Trade Commission issues a fine
B. The Federal Trade Commission goes to court
C. The Federal Trade Commission starts an investigation (correct)
D. The Federal Trade Commission provides a second chance for compliance with the consent decree
Explanation:
The Federal Trade Commission will first want to figure out to what extent the consent decree is not complied with and will start an investigation. The Federal Trade Commission will not go to court or issue a fine immediately. There will likely also not be a second chance.

31. There is a contract between the ad block software company and the customer. What does this contract have to contain?
A. Consideration, acceptance, offer (correct)
B. Offer, terms, value-added
C. Value-added, signature, offer
D. Offer, counteroffer, acceptance
Explanation:
Consideration, acceptance, and offer are the elements that need to be present in a contract.

32. Which of the following is true regarding adequacy decisions in the European Union?
A. The adequacy decisions are issued by the data protection authority
B. An adequacy decision results in not needing data processing agreements anymore
C. Only the data controllers in the country are affected by the adequacy decision
D. Countries can be deemed partly adequate (correct)
Explanation:
Countries can be deemed partly adequate. Take Canada for example, which is partly adequate, meaning the private sector in Canada is deemed adequate and the government is not.

33. Regarding privacy in Canada, which of the following is false?
A. Consent is a valid basis for using personal information
B. Canada is deemed partially adequate
C. The government works under a different privacy law than the private sector
D. The private sector law is the Protection of Personal Information Act (correct)
Explanation:
The privacy law in Canada is the Personal Information Protection and Electronic Documents Act, not the Protection of Personal Information Act.

34. Which of the following is least likely a data breach when processing the personal information of citizens of the European Union?
A. Stolen personal information
B. Lost personal information
C. Illegally processed personal information (correct)
D. A wrongfully addressed email containing personal information
Explanation:
Illegally processed personal information is just that, illegally processed personal information. When an organization processed personal information without a valid legal basis this does not constitute a data breach.

35. Which of the following is least likely true regarding privacy programs?
A. Privacy programs result in increased awareness
B. Privacy programs are required under the General Data Protection Regulation (correct)
C. Privacy programs are sponsored by the CEO
D. The number of privacy incidents will increase
Explanation:
Privacy programs are not required under the General Data Protection Regulation. A privacy program would help with the implementation, but is not required.

36. Which of the following is most important if you have an international vendor processing personal information for your organization?
A. To determine whether a data processing agreement is required (correct)
B. To ensure audit rights
C. To designate personal information for processing within the state only
D. To ensure the bidding process abides by the rules
Explanation:
When using a data processor (a third party processing personal information for you at your request), a data processing agreement is required. This is for good reason, as the data processing agreement specifies the terms of the processing, such as the required security level and where the data is stored.

37. An organization fails to meet the requirements for data collection from children. Which entity is most likely going to take action?
A. The Federal Communications Commission
B. The Federal Trade Commission (correct)
C. The Department of Justice
D. The attorney general
Explanation:
The Federal Trade Commission is the enforcement agency of the Children's Online Privacy Protection Act, and therefore most likely the one taking action.

38. The Children's Online Privacy Protection Act has improved online privacy for children. Which of the following is not required by the Children's Online Privacy Protection Act when using the personal information of children?
A. Express consent
B. Affirmation
C. Opt-in
D. Op-out (correct)
Explanation:
Parents will need to be able to opt out of an organization processing their child's personal information.

39. The Federal Trade Commission was notified of a major unfair practice but is unable to investigate. Which of the following is most likely the case?
A. The Federal Trade Commission does not investigate unfair practices
B. It concerns a deceptive practice instead
C. It concerns a nonprofit organization (correct)
D. It concerns a multinational organization
Explanation:
The Federal Trade Commission cannot investigate certain organizations, this includes nonprofit organizations. Other examples are transportation carriers and financial institutions.

40. At some point, an order issued by the Federal Trade Commission becomes final. After how many days will this be?
A. 90 days
B. 30 days
C. 60 days (correct)
D. 365 days
Explanation:
An order issued by the Federal Trade Commission becomes final 60 days after it is served.

41. Which of the following is false regarding consent decrees?
A. A company does not admit guilt
B. Can lead to enforcement in federal court
C. Consent decrees are the Federal Trade Commission's sole means of enforcement (correct)
D. Consent decrees can apply for up to twenty years
Explanation:
The Federal Trade Commission has more means of privacy enforcement, such as going to court and issuing fines.

42. Which of the following is the best example of an unfair trade practice?
A. Making false claims in a privacy notice
B. Leaving out information in a privacy statement
C. Sharing information with a foreign third party
D. Not implementing adequate security measures (correct)
Explanation:
When an organization implements inadequate security measures, or no security measures at all, this can constitute an unfair trade practice. The actions taken by the Federal Trade Commission, such as against LabMD and Wyndham Worldwide Corporation, show that inadequate security is considered an unfair trade practice.

43. Which of the following is not a requirement for de-identification under the Health Insurance Portability and Accountability Act privacy rule?
A. Encryption of 256-bit when used for medical research (correct)
B. Removing at least 18 data elements
C. Having a certified small risk of re-identification
D. Having a reasonable basis to believe the individuals cannot be identified
Explanation:
There is no specification for the level of encryption in the Health Insurance Portability and Accountability Act privacy rule.

44. During an investigation you find out a list of passwords was accessed by a third party. Which of the following reduces the potential damage done in such an instance the least?
A. If the data was hashed
B. If the data was salted
C. If the data was encrypted
D. If the data was compressed (correct)
Explanation:
If the data was compressed, this means it was made more compact. This has no effect on whether an unauthorized party can access it. In fact, if the file is smaller, it can be copied faster and therefore the third party will need less time.

45. What was an initial goal of the Health Insurance Portability and Accountability Act?
A. Improving the quality of healthcare delivery
B. Improving the efficiency of healthcare delivery (correct)
C. Improving medical privacy practices
D. Improving the security during the handling of medical data
Explanation:
Contrary to what you might expect, the privacy regulation did not have the sole goal to improve privacy but was actually intended to improve the efficiency of healthcare delivery.

Use this case for the next four questions:
Nowadays everything is being recorded all the time. Every car has a dashboard camera, and every cyclist is wearing a camera. One way to wear a camera is on a helmet. Helm-cam is a company that produces the most popular type of helmet camera. From cyclist helmets to motorcycle helmets, the company produces all types.

The cameras can work by simply inserting a micro-SD card into the device. This is inconvenient since the video will have to be copied from the micro-SD card, meaning the micro-SD card needs to be removed from the camera and inserted into a different device. Many users have complained about this inconvenience.

After having listened to its customers' complaints, Helm-cam decided to add two more options to get the video to a different device. The first method works via Bluetooth only. If a user selects this option, the video from the camera will be captured on the phone of the user. This requires less processing power from the camera, improving battery life. The second option involves a Bluetooth connection with the user's phone as well, but instead of storing the video on the user's phone, the video is stored directly in the cloud. The company figured it can charge an extra monthly fee for the use of the cloud space.

Since the company now processes a lot more personal information, namely the videos stored on the cloud, it hires a privacy officer. The privacy officer is put to work right away, as the data breach occurs on his first day. This eventually leads to a court case, as protection proved to be inadequate and customers were informed of the breach too late.

46. You purchased a helmet camera, and it suddenly gives you the option to either render the device useless or accept an invasive new privacy policy. Which entity is most likely going to seek compensation?
A. The Federal Trade Commission (correct)
B. The Federal Communications Commission
C. The Department of Justice
D. The state attorney
Explanation:
This is quite possibly an unfair or deceptive trade practice. Unfair and deceptive trade practices are enforced by the Federal Trade Commission.

47. During the court case, the judge says the case is similar to another case and copies the decision. What is likely the case?
A. Mens rea
B. Stare decisis (correct)
C. Common law
D. Decisis trancendus
Explanation:
Stare decisis is when a current case is decided consistent with a past decision. Mens rea is the requirement for criminal intent.

48. The company incorrectly claims not to collect location data. Which of the following does this likely constitute?
A. A deceptive trade practice (correct)
B. An unfair trade practice
C. The violation of a consent decree
D. A violation of the acceptance of the contract in the form of the privacy notice
Explanation:
When you claim something, and then intentionally do another thing, you are misleading. This constitutes a deceptive trade practice.

49. Your cloud-stored videos have been accessed by an outsider. This happened because you opened a malicious file. Which of the following tort is most likely applicable?
A. Intrusion upon seclusion
B. Trespass to land
C. Invasion of solitude (correct)
D. Intentional infliction of emotional distress
Explanation:
Invasion of solitude is an intrusion into private affairs, physically or electronically. Accessing someone's videos fits this tort.

50. Covered entities are defined in the Transaction Rule, the Privacy Rule, and the Security Rule. In which of these three is the definition of covered entities most strict?
A. The Transaction Rule
B. The Privacy Rule
C. The Security Rule
D. All are equally strict (correct)
Explanation:
All definitions are the same, and therefore equally strict.

51. Which of the following is least likely covered by the 'Confidentiality of Substance Use Disorder Patient Records Rule'?
A. A free psychologist partially specialized in addiction
B. A doctor in a public hospital, specialized in damage to the liver caused by alcohol
C. A substance abuse counselor in a government hospital
D. A person's general practitioner, discussing the issues (correct)
Explanation:
A general practitioner is not specialized in substance abuse treatment, which is a requirement. All other options have a specialization in substance abuse.

52. A data inventory can help organizations see which personal information it uses. Which of the following requires a data inventory?
A. The Children's Online Privacy Protection Act
B. The Gramm-Leach-Bliley Act (correct)
C. The California Online Privacy Protection Act
D. The Fair Credit Reporting Act
Explanation:
Gramm-Leach-Bliley Act Safety Rule requires a data inventory. Another correct answer would be the General Data Protection Regulation, but that is not included in the options.

53. Which of the following contributed the least to the need for the Fair Credit Reporting Act?
A. The increasingly competitive labor market (correct)
B. The increasing importance of consumer credit
C. The increase in inaccurate information
D. The consequences of inaccurate information
Explanation:
The labor market was not of influence to the need for the Fair Credit Reporting Act. Although credit reports can be used in the employment process, the labor market being competitive was not of influence.

54. What is the primary use of consumer reports?
A. Assisting in assessing eligibility for credit (correct)
B. Assisting in the recruitment process
C. Assisting law enforcement agencies
D. Evaluation for opening a bank account
Explanation:
Although there are other uses for consumer reports, they are primarily used to assess eligibility for credit.

55. In case a company fails to properly investigate consumers who attempt to dispute the information in their consumer reports, which of the following is most likely to bring enforcement action?
A. The Consumer Financial Protection Bureau (correct)
B. The Federal Trade Commission
C. State attorneys general
D. The Federal Communications Commission
Explanation:
See the case against Clarity Services. In that case consumers who attempted to dispute the information in their consumer reports were not properly investigated by Clarity Services. The Consumer Financial Protection Bureau was the one bringing enforcement action, and therefore the correct answer here.

56. The Gramm-Leach-Bliley Act privacy rule places requirements on financial institutions. Which of the following is such a requirement?
A. Opting out of joint marketing efforts with third parties
B. Refrain from disclosing personal information to third parties
C. Opting out of having non-public personal information shared with non-affiliated third parties (correct)
D. Provide a monthly update on changes in the privacy notice
Explanation:
People can opt out of having their non-public personal information shared with non-affiliated third parties. Option D would also be correct, but it concerns an annual update and not a monthly update.

57. The parents of a student who is 21 are able to request the student's education records, much to the student's dismay. Which of the following is most likely the case?
A. The student is a dependent for tax purposes (correct)
B. It concerns a foreign exchange student
C. The student is no longer attending the educational institution
D. The student has consented
Explanation:
If a student is a dependent for tax purposes, the parents are able to request the student's education records.

58. Which of the following is not a right provided to students by the Family Educational Rights and Privacy Act?
A. To review and amend their education records (correct)
B. To receive an annual notice of their rights
C. To control disclosure of education records to others
D. To file a complaint
Explanation:
A student cannot amend his/her education records, but can only seek amendment. The complaint filed under option D refers to a complaint filed with the U.S. Department of Education.

59. The Family Educational Rights and Privacy Act has several criteria for consent. Which of the following is not one of the criteria for consent?
A. Records subject to disclosure must be specific
B. The consent must be dated
C. The right to withdraw consent must be specified (correct)
D. The consent cannot be verbal
Explanation:
There is no need to specify the right to withdraw consent. Option D is phrased misleadingly, but is true since consent must be signed in writing.

60. The 'K-12 School Service Provider Pledge to Safeguard Privacy' is which of the following?
A. Sectoral law
B. Federal law
C. Self-regulation (correct)
D. State law
Explanation:
As the title suggests, it is a pledge of school service providers. This is an example of an industry creating its own regulation, which is self-regulation.

61. The way we consume video entertainment has radically changed over the years, and moved to mostly streaming services. Which of the following is not applicable to streaming services?
A. None of the options
B. The General Data Protection Regulation
C. The Video Privacy Protection Act
D. The Cable Communications Policy Act (correct)
Explanation:
As the name suggests, the Cable Communications Policy Act applies only to cable television. It does therefore not apply to video streaming services.

62. Opt-outs are frequently used. In which situation is an opt-out least likely allowed?
A. A 'please call me' button (correct)
B. An 'I do not wish to receive emails' button
C. A 'contact me' box
D. A preferred method of contact box
Explanation:
A 'please call me' button should be an opt-in. The Telemarketing Sales Rule forbids the 'please call me' button to be prechecked, which is the same as forbidding an opt-out mechanism.

Use this case for the next three questions:
An employer in California employs 700 employees. For some levels in the organization it is employment at will, for other groups an employment contract is signed by the employee and the employer. The remuneration the employer offers is quite competitive, and employees are happy to work there, with or without an employment contract.

The company is keen on collecting data on its employees for efficiency improvement analysis. This resulted in data lakes of which less than 5% is actually used in efficiency improvement efforts. Despite having been told that having the data without needing to have it poses a risk to the organization, the CEO does not want to discard the data because 'it might be of use someday'. CCTV images are part of the data collected by the employer. Advanced facial recognition is used to detect which employee is in the image. The software is not advanced enough yet to identify the tasks or actions the employees in the images are performing, but slowly the software is being improved towards that end.

Unions are meddling when it comes to labor conditions. Whenever an improvement for union members can be arranged, the unions are quick to force negotiations with the employer. Up until now, the unions were not aware of the invasiveness of the data-collecting practices of the employer, but at the moment a data analyst is growing a conscience and is preparing to inform the unions of the employer's invasive practices.

63. There is a contract between the company and the employee. What would the job description and the salary be referred to as?
A. Terms
B. Bargain
C. Acceptance
D. Consideration (correct)
Explanation:
The job description is the tasks the employee will perform for money, and from the provided options this most likely contains the consideration. The other elements of a contract are offer and acceptance.

64. The employer scans the emails of its employees. Which type of privacy does this have the biggest impact on?
A. Bodily privacy
B. Territorial privacy
C. Geographic privacy
D. Information privacy (correct)
Explanation:
The best answer here would be communications privacy, but that is not one of the options. Therefore, information privacy fits best and is the correct answer.

65. The employees accuse the employer of excessive video monitoring. Excessive video monitoring is most likely a violation of which class of privacy?
A. Bodily privacy
B. Territorial privacy (correct)
C. Information privacy
D. Communications privacy
Explanation:
Video (without sound) invades your territory as it were. Therefore, this concerns territorial privacy.

66. Which of the following cannot access the National Do Not Call Registry?
A. Sellers
B. Consumers (correct)
C. Telemarketers
D. Service providers of sellers/telemarketers
Explanation:
In order to access the National Do Not Call Registry, you need a Subscription Account Number. Consumers likely do not have a Subscription Account Number.

67. Federal Rule of Civil Procedure 45 contains requirements for subpoenas. Which of the following is not a requirement for a subpoena?
A. A subpoena must be served electronically (correct)
B. A subpoena must contain the civil action number
C. A subpoena must contain the title of the action
D. The person's right to seek modification of the subpoena must be included
Explanation:
Option A is false, and therefore the correct answer. There is no requirement for a subpoena to be served electronically.

68. Which of the following is least likely an exception to attorney-client privilege?
A. The information is pertinent to the case, but the client does not agree to share it (correct)
B. The information will incriminate the client but can save someone's life
C. The information will not incriminate the client and can save someone's life
D. The client agrees to share the information, regardless of it being pertinent to the case
Explanation:
All except for option A are exceptions to attorney-client privilege.

69. Which of the following is least likely true regarding the Electronic Communications Privacy Act and similar laws?
A. Interception is allowed if one of the parties agrees to it in the U.S. (correct)
B. The Electronic Communications Privacy Act resulted in emails falling under the ban on interception
C. Anything over a wire, when privacy can reasonably be expected, is covered
D. An exception is when the interception is done in any ordinary course of business
Explanation:
It depends on the state whether one or all parties need to agree to the interception. Not all states allow interception in case just one party agrees to it.

70. How can you best describe a discovery request?
A. E-discovery in a criminal case
B. A request from a party in a lawsuit (correct)
C. An order by a judge to release information pertinent to the case
D. Similar to a national security letter
Explanation:
A discovery request is where one party in a civil case asks the other party for information. This can be documents or things, questions, or requests for admissions.

71. During litigation, a protective order can be sought. Which of the following best describes a protective order?
A. The removal of a name
B. A whistle-blower procedure
C. Privilege granted, such as spousal privilege
D. Information for an attorney's eyes only (correct)
Explanation:
If a protective order is sought and granted by the court, personal information is redacted by the attorney when filing documents to the court. This pertains to social security numbers and other sensitive information. Therefore, the information can be said to be for the attorney's eyes only.

72. Workplace privacy can be tricky. Which of the following is least likely true regarding workplace privacy?
A. The General Data Protection Regulation can be applicable in the U.S. workplace
B. Employers have an incentive to collect a lot of personal information on their (prospective) employees
C. There are laws that require the collection of personal information before hiring an employee
D. The European Union has more laws providing employee privacy than the U.S. (correct)
Explanation:
The European Union has one main law, the General Data Protection Regulation, which is quite comprehensive. The U.S. on the other hand, has several laws which are not comprehensive, even combined.

73. In the U.S., employees are generally employed using employment at will. Which of the following can provide the greatest privacy protection?
A. The General Data Protection Regulation
B. Collective bargaining agreements (correct)
C. Local state law
D. Background check laws
Explanation:
If unions enter into collective bargaining agreements, labor conditions influencing privacy can be included. Therefore, in the context of an employer in the U.S. (not the European Union), option B is the correct answer. The other options can also provide privacy protection, but not to the extent collective bargaining agreements potentially can.

74. The Department of Labor administers several laws. Which of the following is not administered by the Department of Labor?
A. The Age Discrimination in Employment Act (correct)
B. The Occupational Safety and Health Act
C. The Fair Labor Standards Act
D. The Employee Retirement Income Security Act
Explanation:
The Age Discrimination in Employment Act is administered by the Department of Labor. The other laws are not.

75. Employers often overstep privacy boundaries. Which of the following is least likely forbidden at an office?
A. Closed-circuit television in the locker room
B. Closed-circuit television in the restroom
C. Opening an employee's personal mail (correct)
D. Listening in on personal phone conversations
Explanation:
If the employee receives personal mail at work, the employer is allowed to open it. The requirement here is that the mail is sent to the employee's work address.

76. Which of the following is most likely true for HR-related privacy issues?
A. HR-related privacy issues are overshadowed by consumer privacy risks for traditional organizations
B. Employment at will reduces the risk of HR-related privacy issues
C. The introduction of IT resulted in HR-related privacy issues requiring attention
D. HR-related privacy issues form a risk to all organizations (correct)
Explanation:
There were significant HR-related privacy issues before the introduction of IT, whether consumer privacy risks overshadow HR-related privacy risks cannot be claimed, and employment at will does not reduce HR-related privacy risks. Therefore, D is the correct answer.

77. In the U.S. several laws forbid discrimination in employment. Which of the following could be a valid reason to discriminate?
A. Consent of the candidate or employee regarding the use of the personal information on the basis of which discrimination takes place
B. Discrimination based on pregnancy revealed after a voluntary drug test
C. An employer found out through a mutual acquaintance that an employee handling finances has filed for bankruptcy
D. Not hiring a disabled person for manual work (correct)
Explanation:
If the job description includes tasks that the candidate cannot perform, even when adjustments are made, an employer does not violate anti-discrimination laws by not hiring that candidate. Not qualified is not qualified, regardless of whether a person is disabled.

78. During employment, employers cannot use lie detectors. Which of the following is not an example of a lie detector?
A. Email analyses (correct)
B. Polygraphs
C. Voice stress analyzers
D. Psychological stress evaluators
Explanation:
Email analysis least likely constitutes a lie detector. Of course, you can analyze emails for contradicting messages, or patterns that indicate lies, but the other three options are more conventional lie detector tests.

79. Data loss prevention can be of great value when trying to detect when employees sneak out sensitive data. Which of the following is not an element of a successful data loss prevention program?
A. Data governance
B. Data discovery
C. Training and awareness
D. A legal basis (correct)
Explanation:
You might need a legal basis to perform certain data loss prevention monitoring, but it is not part of a data loss prevention program. If you need a legal basis to work with certain personal information, you should already have the legal basis before starting the data loss prevention program.

Use this case for the next three questions:
Fair trade coffee is increasing in popularity due to the growing awareness amongst consumers of the consequences of unfair trade. Not only has this led to the bigger coffee producers increasing fairness in their supply chain and using that as a selling point in their advertisement, but farms in coffee-producing countries also started selling their coffee online through coffee traders.

One coffee trader allows consumers to order coffee from the farmer of their choosing, using the coffee trader as a middleman. The coffee trader even placed photos and profiles of the local farmers on its website, including a live video feed if the farmers has put up cameras on his coffee plantation.

After ordering through the coffee trader, something called a 'flavor preference profile' is created, and the consumer is informed regularly by email about harvests that fit the customer's flavor preference profile. There is no possibility of opting out, which customers do not seem to mind.

On top of the regular emailing, the coffee trader attempts to reach its larger customers by phone from time to time in order to secure larger sales. Although some of these larger customers are individuals, they order suspiciously large amounts of coffee, which the coffee trader chooses to ignore. The coffee trader even receives large cash payments from time to time, which does not seem to worry the coffee trader.

80. The coffee trader extends credit to some of its customers but does not use consumer reports. Which of the following is most likely true for the coffee trader?
A. The coffee trader will need to implement a red flag program (correct)
B. The personal information processed will have to comply with stricter requirements
C. The personal information processed will fall within the scope of the General Data Protection Regulation
D. Consumers will have the same access rights to the personal information used as with consumer reports
Explanation:
If an organization extends credit, the Fair Credit Reporting Act requires that a red flag program is implemented, despite the organization not making use of consumer reports. The red flag program is meant to detect/deter identity theft.

81. An affiliate of the coffee trader can transfer personal information from the EU under an adequacy decision, but the government cannot. In which country is the affiliate located?
A. Canada (correct)
B. Israel
C. New Zealand
D. Japan
Explanation:
The private sector in Canada is deemed adequate, and the government is not.

82. The trader calls customers who placed themselves on the National Do Not Call Registry. How long ago can these customers have made their previous purchase?
A. Maximum 16 months ago
B. Maximum 20 months ago
C. Maximum 18 months ago (correct)
D. Maximum 12 months ago
Explanation:
The purchase, rental, or lease has to have occurred within 18 months. If you encounter a similar question where none of the options is 18 months, choose the one closest (but less than 18 months).

83. Which of the following is true regarding federal versus state privacy laws?
A. State law generally preempts federal law
B. Federal law never preempts state law
C. State laws specify whether federal law preempts it
D. Federal law generally preempts state law (correct)
Explanation:
There are only a few federal laws that allow stricter state laws to preempt.

84. Which law amends the California Consumer Privacy Act?
A. The California FTC Act
B. The California Privacy Amendment Act
C. The California Privacy Rights Act (correct)
D. The Federal Communications Committee California rules of procedure
Explanation:
The California Privacy Rights Act amends the California Consumer Privacy Act. The other options either do not exist (B and D) or are at the federal level (A).

85. Which of the following is not true under Nevada SB 538?
A. All websites in Nevada are required to post a privacy policy (correct)
B. The privacy policy needs to contain the effective date
C. The privacy policy needs to contain a process for correcting personally identifiable information
D. Web hosting services are excluded from liabilities for violations
Explanation:
Option A is not true, since non-commercial websites or those with fewer than 20.000 visitors do not need to post a privacy policy.

86. The California Privacy Rights Act grants consumers certain rights. Which of the following is such a right granted under the California Privacy Rights Act?
A. The right to opt out
B. The right to correction (correct)
C. The right to know
D. The right to access
Explanation:
The right to correction is granted under the California Privacy Rights Act.

87. Under the California Consumer Privacy Act, it can be requested to delete certain personal information. If a company refuses to delete your personal information, which of the following is least likely the case?
A. The company has a contract with a third party involving the personal information (correct)
B. The company has to complete a transaction requiring your personal information
C. The company is investigating fraud and your personal information is crucial to the investigation
D. For tax reporting requirements, your personal information needs to remain with the company for a certain period
Explanation:
A contract with a third party cannot influence whether your personal information is deleted or not (unless perhaps you consented to this). The other options do make sense, especially if your personal information is required to complete a transaction, for example sending you the products you have ordered.

88. Which of the following is most likely going to reduce the risk of non-compliance with state privacy law?
A. Hiring a privacy officer
B. Appointing a data protection officer
C. Applying role-based access control
D. Collecting only the personal information needed to conduct business (correct)
Explanation:
Collecting only the personal information required is always a good strategy, to comply with any privacy law. Of course, the other options can have a positive effect, but they are likely less effective and on top of that they are reactive.

89. Under California's AB 1950, which of the following, in combination with a person's name, would least likely constitute a data breach if leaked?
A. Debit card number
B. Telephone number (correct)
C. Driver's license number
D. Automated license plate recognition information
Explanation:
Telephone numbers that are leaked do not constitute a data breach under California's AB 1950. If you did not know the answer, you could have reasoned that this was the least sensitive element among the options.

90. States have enacted breach notification laws. Which state was the first to do so?
A. North Carolina
B. California (correct)
C. New York
D. Florida
Explanation:
California was the first. This is a useless fact, but if you got this one correct, good for you.

Exam 3:

1. A brand new federal law imposing privacy requirements has been drafted. Which party has the last word when it comes to accepting the law?
A. The house of representatives
D. The president
C. Congress
D. The supreme court

2. A brand new law has been accepted, granting some freedom as regards personal information to organizations. Which party has the last word when it comes to adhering to the law?
A. The Federal Trade Commission
B. The U.S. supreme court
C. The legislative branch
D. The president

3. Which of the following laws contains private right of action?
A. The Gramm-Leach-Bliley Act
B. The Health Insurance Portability and Accountability Act
C. The Family Educational Rights and Privacy Act
D. The California Consumer Privacy Act

4. Circuit courts are appealed to after a lower court. How many circuit courts are there?
A. 94
B. 13
C. 50
D. 23

5. Which of the following is true regarding privacy and the U.S. Constitution?
A. The U.S. Constitution arguably does not provide any privacy protection
B. Privacy is not explicitly mentioned, but the right to be let alone is
C. The U.S. Constitution arguably provides implicit privacy protection
D. There can never be explicit privacy protection in the U.S. Constitution

6. The 'code of federal regulations' is administrative law. Which of the following is true regarding administrative law?
A. The Health Insurance Portability and Accountability Act privacy rule is not an example of administrative law
B. Administrative law does not have to go through the legislative process
C. The Health Insurance Portability and Accountability Act security rule is not an example of administrative law
D. Administrative law is based on case law

7. A court does not always have authority over the parties involved. Which of the following is missing in such a case?
A. Subject matter authority
B. A contract between the parties involved
C. Relevant case law
D. Personal jurisdiction

8. You make use of private right of action a federal law provides. Which of the following is the second court you appeal to?
A. The U.S. supreme court
B. A district court
C. A circuit court
D. The district attorney

9. Which of the following is least likely true regarding contract law?
A. Contracts are not always legally binding
B. Only the parties of the contract are legally liable
C. When a contract violates a law, it is not enforceable in court
D. There must be mutual intent to be bound

10. The General Data Protection Regulation applies to the personal information processing of the European Union's citizens, and under certain conditions even if the personal information is processed in other countries. What can you most applicably call the General Data Protection Regulation also applying in the U.S.?
A. Scope
B. Application
C. Jurisdiction
D. EU-US Privacy Shield

11. There are several types of liability. How would you describe the difference between criminal and civil liability?
A. Civil liability is about a crime having affected the respondent
B. Criminal liability is about a crime having affected the claimant
C. Civil liability involves mens rea, and criminal liability involves a defendant
D. Civil liability involves a claimant and criminal liability involves the government

12. Which of the following is not part of negligence or invasion of privacy?
A. Mens rea
B. Duty of care
C. Damages
D. False light

13. Anonymization is not exactly the same as de-identification. Which of the following best describes the differences?
A. Anonymization requires using pseudonyms, de-identification requires the removal of identifiers
B. Anonymization needs to be done by an external expert, de-identification can be done in-house
C. Anonymization is irreversible, whereas de-identification is not necessarily irreversible
D. De-identification is stricter than anonymization

Use this case for the next four questions:
A new indie rock band has released its debut album without being signed by a major record label. This is not by choice, but more because none of the record labels that the band contacted were interested. The independent release of a record means more intense contact with the (yet-to-be-formed) fanbase. Although concerts are generally well attended, the band suspects this to be due to the other bands that perform the same evening, so this deserves some attention.

When the band performs, digital interactive art is incorporated into the music. This involves images being made of the attendees and incorporated into the images projected onto the screen. The band enjoys this process, even though the concertgoers do not seem to pay too much attention to the art. As a memento, the band stores all images and final art on an external hard drive.

The band's music is solely available online. No CDs or vinyl are available with the band's music. This fits the band's philosophy of reducing waste. Although the main music streaming services do not carry the band's music, the band has set up an online purchase system where customers can download a song after purchasing it, or stream it and pay a smaller fee every time the customer listens to the song. The sales data is then analyzed by the band, after which the conclusion is reached that people do not buy the song after streaming it (or even stream it again), hence in order to optimize profits the band disables the option to stream the songs.

14. If the website did not contain a privacy policy or information on the privacy practices, which Fair Information Practice Principle is most likely violated?
A. Collection
B. Data subject access
C. Information quality
D. Disclosure and notice

15. The band's website does have a privacy policy. However, you later find out that more personal information was collected than was mentioned in the website's privacy policy. Which of the following is most likely true?
A. The Federal Trade Commission can assess civil penalties
B. The Federal Communications Commission can ask the website to enter into a consent decree
C. The Federal Trade Commission can seek compensation
D. The scenario is neither deceptive nor unfair

16. The band sends out regular emails to inform its mailing list consisting of customers and addresses acquired through a data broker. The emails contain information on new merchandise and discounts. Which of the following is required for those emails according to the Controlling the Assault of Non-Solicited Pornography And Marketing Act?
A. Opt-out
B. Opt-in
C. Sent at certain times only
D. Use a .com email address

17. When sending emails to a mailing list some recipients might want to be removed from the mailing list. Which of the following is true regarding the removal from the mailing list?
A. The person opting out can be required to show a form of identification
B. A fee can be charged for processing costs
C. The General Data Protection Regulation applies to mailing lists, which grants the right to be forgotten
D. Opting out can be allowed by phone

18. The Golden State Killer was finally caught after many years, through DNA. Which type of privacy was sacrificed to catch him?
A. Territorial privacy
B. Communications privacy
C. Information privacy
D. Bodily privacy

19. A hardcopy file that includes personal information has been stolen. In which of the following states is that personal information most likely covered under the state's breach notification law?
A. California
B. New Orleans
C. Georgia
D. Hawaii

20. Websites in the European Union are required to communicate certain information about how they deal with personal information. Of which Fair Information Practice Principle is this an example?
A. Choice and consent
B. Use and retention
C. Data subject access
D. Notice

21. When a large organization fails to inform a person on which other organizations his/her personal information is shared with, which Fair Information Practice Principle is most likely violated?
A. Disclosure and notice
B. Collection limitation
C. Choice
D. Security safeguards

22. Privacy by Design is a concept embedded in certain laws. Which of the following type of cookies lends itself least to Privacy by Design?
A. Tracking cookies
B. Flash cookies
C. Functional cookies
D. Analytical cookies

23. Ever since the General Data Protection Regulation came into force, organizations are giving privacy more attention and many are implementing a privacy program. Which of the following is least likely in charge of the implementation of such a privacy program?
A. The data protection officer
B. The privacy officer
C. The CEO
D. A designated privacy program manager

24. Data breaches can require prompt action, and even external communication. Who is generally responsible if a data breach response is inadequate?
A. The organization's data protection officer
B. The organization's chief security officer
C. The organization's privacy officer
D. The organization's CEO

25. Employee training can benefit an organization. Which of the following is least likely true regarding employee training?
A. Employee training reduces security incidents
B. Data breaches are detected faster
C. The privacy of both employees and customers improves
D. Employee training ensures compliance

26. Which of the following is least likely true in the case of a data breach involving a data processor?
A. The data processor has to inform the data subjects
B. An investigation needs to be initiated by the data controller
C. If the data processor breached the contract, it can be held accountable
D. The data protection authority needs to be informed

27. Organizations cannot keep personal information forever. Which of the following is not a consideration for determining the retention period of personal information?
A. Whether the personal information has served its purpose
B. Available storage space
C. The legal requirements
D. The completion of the processes using the personal information

28. Which of the following is most likely false regarding the international use of personal information?
A. When multiple organizations are involved, a contract is needed
B. Data inventories are done for the whole chain
C. Public personal information does not need protection
D. When transferring personal information to a third party, there needs to be a legal basis to do so

29. Which of the following is the best strategy for international privacy law compliance?
A. Apply Binding Corporate Rules
B. Comply with the Fair Information Practice Principles
C. Appoint a privacy officer
D. Ask for consent before collecting personal information

30. Which of the following is an important privacy by design consideration when developing a global IT system?
A. That the data protection officer has the highest level of access
B. That the chief information security officer has the highest level of access
C. That consent can be withdrawn
D. That the IT system is properly tested

31. Which of the following is most likely true regarding the retention period of personal information?
A. A purpose of personal information can be changed, and the retention period can be extended without consent
B. The Family Educational Rights and Privacy Act contains a retention period for directory information
C. Personal information is required to be deleted after the retention period is over
D. The General Data Protection Regulation contains specific retention periods for types of personal information

32. You receive personal information from an affiliate in the European Union with a special addition to the contract. Which of the following is false?
A. The contract constitutes a model contract
B. The contract constitutes Binding Corporate Rules
C. The contract constitutes standard contractual clauses
D. Only the personal information specified in the contract is protected

Use this case for the next three questions:
With the introduction of smartphones, many applications have been developed. Installing these applications requires just a few touches of the screen. This includes many games as well, most of them not age-restricted. One of these games is a colorful video game in which you play a dinosaur collecting bones and rocks. It has become quite popular, and children in schools all over the U.S. are boasting about their high scores.

The game itself is constantly being developed. Most of the development effort goes into adding new looks for the dinosaurs and new levels. Although the game is free to download and play, new additions to the game need to be purchased. These can be purchased within the game, without the need to add a credit card number every time. This is made possible due to blanket permission in the terms and conditions, which most people merely skim or skip.

Parents are furious since they are generally the ones installing the game. In addition, the credit card number is taken from the app store and has not been entered into the game, creating the impression that there is no possibility to charge for anything that is done in the game. The game is designed in a way so that it is difficult to progress without the purchase of at least some upgrades.

Another stream of revenue is generated through analysis of how the players react to triggers in the game and how they interact with certain elements. Insight into this is provided to researchers at a large university, which pays a fee to the video game company.
The game also contains in-game advertisements, where the player is shown an advertisement between levels based on the profile created for that player. There is the option to remove the advertisement, but that option will need to be purchased.

33. The company implements a privacy program to improve the player's privacy. Which of the following is the most likely starting point?
A. A data inventory
B. A data flow map
C. Raising employee awareness and involvement
D. Hiring a privacy officer

34. Privacy programs such as the one implemented by the company generally contain several elements. Which of the following is the least likely part of a privacy program?
A. A data breach response procedure
B. An employee training program
C. Hiring privacy staff
D. A data loss prevention campaign

35. The company found out a data breach occurred and player data was leaked. When is the company going to report it?
A. At the most expedient time, without unreasonable delay
B. Immediately after discovering a security incident occurred
C. When the investigation into the incident has finished
D. When the company finds out it has a legal responsibility to notify

36. Data breaches can require notifying certain parties. Which of the following will least likely need to be notified in case of a data breach?
A. Someone whose encrypted medical data was lost
B. Someone who was supposed to receive an email, but it was inadvertently sent to the wrong person
C. The state attorney general
D. Someone's personal information crucial to a service was accidentally deleted

37. Which of the following is the most important consideration when storing personal information on a cloud server?
A. What type of personal information will be stored
B. Where the personal information will be physically stored
C. The encryption method used
D. Whether you are the data controller or the data processor

38. Which of the following is most relevant for role-based access control?
A. Data classification
B. Storage location
C. Data flow diagram
D. Filetype

39. What did the Schrems II case result in?
A. An adequacy decision being repealed
B. Canada's private sector being considered adequate
C. Limitations in the use of Binding Corporate Rules
D. EU-US Privacy Shield being declared void

40. In California there are limitations on the use of social security numbers. Which of the following is least likely forbidden to do with social security numbers?
A. Transmission over Hypertext Transfer Protocol
B. Printing on tax forms/letters
C. Including the number on an ID card
D. Displaying on a gym membership card

41. Which of the following is true regarding the Federal Trade Commission's role?
A. The Federal Trade Commission concerns itself with computer security issues
B. The president has direct control over the Federal Trade Commission
C. Section 6 of the FTC Act is the most important piece of U.S. privacy law
D. The Federal Trade Commission started enforcing privacy issues in the recent years

42. To which of the following is the Federal Trade Commission's authority from section 5 of the Federal Trade Commission Act most likely applicable?
A. A bank
B. A transportation company
C. A communications company
D. A retailer

43. Which of the following is least likely going to happen if there are several minor problems in an organization's privacy practices brought to the attention of the Federal Trade Commission?
A. The Federal Trade Commission will enter into a consent decree with the company
B. The Federal Trade Commission will launch an investigation into the issues
C. The Federal Trade Commission will work with the company to resolve the problems
D. The Federal Trade Commission will start an administrative trial

44. The Federal Trade Commission can seek penalties. Which of the following is true regarding the Federal Trade Commission seeking penalties?
A. The Federal Trade Commission can seek penalties in a district court, up to $43 280
B. The Federal Trade Commission can seek penalties in federal court, up to $43 280
C. The Federal Trade Commission can seek penalties in a district court, up to $38 180
D. The Federal Trade Commission can seek penalties in federal court, up to $38 180

45. Which of the following does not contain requirements for privacy notices?
A. The Health Insurance Portability and Accountability Act
B. The Gramm-Leach-Bliley Act
C. The Children's Online Privacy Protection Act
D. The Federal Trade Commission Act

46. What is the Federal Trade Commission's approach under chairman Robert Pitofsky also referred to as?
A. The consent approach
B. The transparency approach
C. The Fair Information Practice Principles approach
D. The notice and choice approach

47. IP addresses can, under certain circumstances, be traced back to an individual. In which of the following situations is an IP address most likely considered personal information?
A. In case of a breach of healthcare information
B. When an unsecured Hypertext Transfer Protocol is used
C. In case a virtual private network is used
D. In case a computer is shared

48. Which of the following statements concerning the Health Insurance Portability and Accountability Act is false?
A. The Health Insurance Portability and Accountability Act is updated by The Health Information Technology for Economic and Clinical Health Act
B. The Health Insurance Portability and Accountability Act is not applicable when payment is in cash
C. The Health Insurance Portability and Accountability Act preempts state law
D. The Health Insurance Portability and Accountability Act does not prevent medical research

49. Which of the following is the most suitable definition of personal health information falling under the Health Insurance Portability and Accountability Act?
A. Information that can be traced back to a single individual
B. Any individually identifiable health information transmitted or maintained
C. Any medical information in electronic form, pertaining to a single individual
D. Any information held by covered entities

50. Covered entities are required to provide a privacy notice in most cases. Which of the following would least likely have to provide a privacy notice?
A. A general practitioner
B. A radiologist
C. A specialist
D. A plastic surgeon

Use this case for the next three questions:
An online casino has been increasingly successful during a recent pandemic that resulted in many locations having to close for the duration of the pandemic. Its clientele used to consist of those gambling occasionally but has now expanded to those who used to frequent casinos when they were still open.

When a customer signs up on the casino's website, credit needs to be purchased. Depending on the amount of credit purchased, the online casino runs a background check. This takes several forms and is mainly to prevent reputational damage in case of any suspected criminal ties of the customer.

Recently, the casino started providing free kids games. This is intended to introduce children to casino games like poker so that in their later years they have a tie with the casino and will keep gambling. There is no payment required whatsoever, nor are there in-game purchases. The only thing required is an account of the parent or guardian, which the child uses to play teddy bear poker and black Jack the kangaroo.

At some point, the database with users, passwords, and all other user data is stolen and sold on the dark web. This leads to many users being exposed as gamblers, having consequences in both family life and professional life, since employers and spouses are shocked by the gambling behavior of some users.

51. The casino places a cookie that stores the browsing history, but only from the moment of placing the cookie. What is this called?
A. An analytical cookie
B. A third-party cookie
C. A flash cookie
D. A tracking cookie

52. The casino also uses credit reports. After the casino completes its purposes for the consumer report it collected, it needs to dispose of the consumer report in accordance with the disposal rule. Which of the following is the least suitable method?
A. Pulverizing
B. Compression
C. Erasing
D. Hiring a document destruction contractor

53. User preferences are becoming increasingly important, and the casino started to pay attention. Which of the following least likely relates to user preferences?
A. Functional cookies
B. Analytical cookies
C. Opt-in
D. Opt-out

54. The Genetic Information Nondiscrimination Act contains exceptions in which employers can request genetic information. Which of the following is not one of the exceptions?
A. It is required to comply with an Occupational Safety and Health Act requirement
B. Contaminated DNA needs to be detected
C. The employer purchased it from a public third party
D. The genetic material is not used for discrimination

55. There are certain required elements in order for something to be considered a consumer report. Which of the following is not such a requirement?
A. Credit history
B. Mode of living
C. Character
D. General reputation

56. Which of the following is not true regarding the Fair and Accurate Credit Transactions Act and the Fair Credit Reporting Act?
A. The Fair and Accurate Credit Transactions Act amended the Fair Credit Reporting Act
B. The Fair and Accurate Credit Transactions Act added provisions related to identity theft
C. The Fair and Accurate Credit Transactions Act introduced prescreening
D. The Fair and Accurate Credit Transactions Act was not the first amendment of the Fair Credit Reporting Act

57. Which of the following elements are you least likely to find in a consumer report?
A. Character
B. General reputation
C. Mode of living
D. Driving history

58. Violations of the Fair Credit Reporting Act can lead to having to pay a penalty. What is the maximum penalty for willful violations?
A. $10 063
B. $1 063
C. $5 063
D. $4 063

59. The Fair and Accurate Credit Transactions Act added a number of consumer protections. Which of the following is not one of those protections?
A. It gave the right to request a free annual consumer report
B. It gave consumers the right the redact the information in their consumer report
C. Credit card numbers need to be truncated
D. Debit card numbers need to be truncated

60. The Gramm-Leach-Bliley Act Safeguard rule imposed several levels of security. Which of the following is not one of those three levels?
A. Administrative security
B. Technical security
C. Organizational security
D. Physical security

61. The Family Educational Rights and Privacy Act is limited to educational institutes which receive federal funding. How is the Family Educational Rights and Privacy Act also known?
A. The Educational Privacy Act
B. The Buckley Amendment
C. The National School Amendment
D. The Clinton Amendment

62. Which of the following is the best definition of 'education record' under the Family Educational Rights and Privacy Act?
A. Any academic achievement and/or result stored in the school's records, either digital or physical
B. Any academic achievement stored in a record of the education institution, except athletic achievements
C. Any record maintained on a student, including applicant records
D. Any record maintained by the school directly related to a student

63. A complaint can be filed if parents or students think their rights have been violated under the Family Educational Rights and Privacy Act. Which of the following investigates the complaint?
A. The Family Policy Compliance Officer
B. The Federal Trade Commission
C. The Federal Communications Commission
D. The Department of Justice

64. Which of the following is false regarding the Telemarketing Sales Rule?
A. The Telemarketing Sales Rule was issued by the Federal Trade Commission
B. Requests to call back must be respected
C. Call only between 8 am and 8 pm
D. Records need to be retained for at least 24 hours

65. Which of the following is true regarding caller ID information and the Telemarketing Sales Rule?
A. The telemarketer must submit its own name and phone number
B. Telemarketers are liable when caller ID information does not reach the customer
C. If the calling equipment does not support caller ID, then the telemarketer can provide this information verbally
D. The phone number used to call may be substituted with the customer-service phone number

66. When is a seller not allowed to call a person part of the National Do Not Call Registry?
A. When it concerns a prospect
B. When it concerns a customer
C. When the customer bought its product less than two years ago
D. When the person inquired about the seller's goods two months ago

67. In which of the following cases is it least likely allowed for law enforcement to perform interceptions?
A. The police expect an email to be sent at a certain time and intercept it
B. The communication is transmitted between two computers only, and not sent over a public network
C. Somehow the owner of the computer agreed to intercepting his/her computer's transmissions
D. The detective leading the investigation has one serious suspect and wants to see the messages sent to other potential suspects

Use this case for the next three questions:
An online dating application is focused on the safety of its users. This has resulted in many features, such as video calling before going on a date, indicating that a date is going to happen with a specific person so that the police can be informed in case something happens. Users have to consent to all this access in certain regions since it can be considered quite invasive.

The latest feature of the dating application is only available for a high fee. This feature allows users to run the profile through an internet sweep using facial recognition. Not only will this confirm the name the users provided, but this will also lead to revealing any scandals the user was involved in.

Using the dating application's latest feature has led to the exposure of many fake profiles used to scam lonely people out of money. Many websites with exposed profiles have appeared, and the occasional documentary is made about the biggest fish in the scammer pool.

Some of the persons listed on the scammer websites are not actually scammers. This is due to inaccuracies in the facial recognition software used by the dating application and disgruntled ex-partners falsely listing someone as a scammer.

A lawsuit was started by one of the persons accused of scamming, claiming the dating application falsely exposed them to be scammers. This leads to a lot of publicity, and the dating application does not want to settle since it claims it did not break any laws.

68. The company intends to restrict certain information from certain types of employees. How is this best done?
A. Metadata policy
B. Encryption
C. Specifying access in a policy
D. Role-based access control

69. Which of the following is least likely involved in the process of releasing information during litigation?
A. The CEO
B. Lawyers
C. IT professionals
D. Privacy professionals

70. The company has made an inventory of which personal information is sent where, all throughout the organization. What is this most likely called?
A. A data inventory
B. A processing agreement
C. A data flow map
D. Binding corporate rules

71. One party of the lawsuit invokes the Hague convention. What is that party most likely trying to do?
A. Force the other party to comply with international e-discovery
B. Redact a large chunk of data in the discovery procedure
C. Displace the Federal Rules of Civil Procedure
D. Allow the General Data Protection Regulation to take precedence over U.S. laws

72. Section 215 of the USA PATRIOT Act has received a lot of attention due to a whistleblower's revelations. Which of the following did that concern?
A. The overruling of the USA FREEDOM Act
B. A large data breach covered up by government officials
C. Targeted collection of call details
D. A database created by the National Security Agency

73. Which of the following created a group of independent experts called amicus curiae?
A. The USA PATRIOT Act
B. The Foreign Intelligence Surveillance Act
C. The USA FREEDOM Act
D. The Federal Trade Commission Act

74. Rule 5.2 of the Federal Rules of Civil Procedure requires attorneys to redact documents before being included in court filings. Which of the following is not such a requirement?
A. The date of birth is redacted to the year of birth
B. For minors, only the initials are included
C. The social security number is redacted to the first four digits
D. Financial account numbers are reduced to the last four digits

75. Workplace privacy in the U.S. is affected by several laws. Which of the following affects the smallest number of people?
A. Tort law
B. The U.S. Constitution
C. The Consolidated Omnibus Budget Reconciliation Act
D. The Employee Retirement Income Security Act

76. Workplace privacy is not gained from just one law. Which of the following is the least likely source of workplace privacy in the U.S.?
A. Health and safety laws
B. Security laws
C. Employee benefit laws
D. Anti-discrimination laws

77. A job applicant declines to authorize a consumer report and is rejected. Which of the following is most likely true?
A. The Fair and Accurate Credit Transactions Act prohibits this
B. The Fair Credit Reporting Act prohibits this
C. Neither the Fair Credit Reporting Act nor the Fair and Accurate Credit Transactions Act prohibits this
D. Both the Fair and Accurate Credit Transactions Act and the Fair Credit Reporting Act prohibit this

78. Criminal background checks are often required. For which of the following is a criminal background check most likely required?
A. For employees from abroad
B. For Health and Safety professionals
C. For persons working with children
D. Persons working with heavy machinery

79. The Americans with Disabilities Act creates restrictions that influence the hiring process. Which of the following can most likely discriminate against 'a qualified individual with a disability because of the disability of such individual'?
A. A factory, where the manager thinks hiring a disabled person might upset the rest of the workers
B. An office manager, not wanting to make the office wheelchair accessible
C. A shop owner, afraid the disability causes absence disrupting business
D. A company where being part of the corporate baseball team is an unofficial part of the job

80. Lie detector tests are quite invasive. Which of the following is true regarding lie detector tests in the workplace?
A. An employee may refuse to take a lie detector test, but the employer may interpret the refusal as a negative sign
B. An employee can refuse to take a lie detector test and the employer cannot punish the employee
C. Employment at will allows for an employer to fire an employee who refuses a lie detector test
D. In case taking a lie detector test is required to judge an employee's character rather than investigate an offense, it can be required

81. Which of the following is least likely restricted under the Washington Biometric Privacy law HB 1493?
A. A driver's license
B. An implanted chip
C. Nose dimensions
D. Freckle pattern

82. Which of the following is not true under the New Jersey Personal Information and Privacy Protection Act?
A. Retailers may only retain limited information from a customer's ID
B. A retailer can collect specific ID information to detect repeat customers
C. Information from an ID card can only be collected if it falls under one of the allowed purposes
D. A violation can result in having to pay $2 500

83. A company is subject to a rule in a regulation to implement the California Privacy Rights Act. Which of the following most likely created the rule in question?
A. The Federal Trade Commission
B. The California Consumer Privacy Protection Agency
C. The Federal Communications Commission
D. The state attorney general

Use this case for the next two questions:
A museum's newest exhibition includes a large number of interactive digital projects. This results in the art being different at every visit, which attracts visitors from all over the country.

One piece of art involves a camera allowing the visitor to manipulate a digital sculpture in real-time through gestures made in front of the camera. A print-out can then be emailed to the visitor if an email address is provided. Unbeknownst to the visitors, all these images are stored by the creator of the art.

Another piece of art scans the visitor and then manipulates the image to let the visitor see how he or she would have looked in the different periods of time, ranging from the prehistoric ages to the 1990s. This piece of art allows for the option to post the generated images on social media, as long as a specific hashtag is used to link the image to the exhibition.

84. If the museum contracts a third party to perform a task involving the personal information generated in the art exhibition, what is that third party?
A. A data controller
B. A co-controller
C. A data subject
D. A data processor

85. The museum has a contract with each of the artists that display their work. A disagreement arises, and the museum goes to court to force the artist to comply with the terms of the contract. A judge decides not to enforce the contract between the company and the artist. Which of the following is most likely the case?
A. The consideration is disproportionate
B. The offer is disproportionate
C. The contract violates a law
D. The counterparty cannot uphold the contract

86. Which of the following is most likely going to result in data destruction compliance?
A. Encrypting personal information irreversibly, after the collection purposes have been fulfilled
B. An organization with a role-based access control policy
C. Implementing physical controls to prevent unauthorized access
D. Deleting personal information from company backups

87. Which of the following is not a requirement under the California Consumer Privacy Act for it to apply?
A. The organization has an annual gross revenue of $25 million
B. 50% or more of annual revenue due to the sale of personal information
C. The organization is located in California
D. The organization shares the personal information of 50 000 or more consumers for commercial purposes

88. In Massachusetts, which of the following is least likely required when processing a name and sensitive data element under 201CMR17 "Standards for the protection of personal information of residents of the Commonwealth"?
A. Allow data subject access
B. Appoint a person to be responsible for information security
C. Monitor the effectiveness of security measures
D. Restrict physical access to the personal information

89. All states have enacted breach notification laws. Which of the following are you least likely to find in these laws?
A. Information on whom to notify
B. The threshold for having to notify
C. Whether to notify the state attorney general
D. The role of the privacy officer

90. Regardless of in which state a data breach takes place, action is likely required. In response to a data breach, which of the following is the least important to consider?
A. The legal basis under which the personal information was collected and stored
B. Which laws are applicable
C. What is considered to be personal information
D. The location of the cloud server

Answer key exam 3:

1C, 2B, 3D, 4B, 5C, 6B, 7D, 8A, 9A, 10C, 11D, 12A, 13C, 14D, 15C, 16A, 17D, 18D, 19D, 20D, 21A, 22B, 23A, 24D, 25D, 26A, 27B, 28C, 29B, 30C, 31C, 32B, 33C, 34D, 35A, 36A, 37B, 38A, 39D, 40B, 41A, 42D, 43C, 44B, 45D, 46D, 47A, 48C, 49B, 50B, 51D, 52B, 53A, 54D, 55A, 56C, 57D, 58D, 59B, 60C, 61B, 62D, 63A, 64C, 65D, 66C, 67B, 68D, 69A, 70C, 71C, 72D, 73C, 74C, 75B, 76B, 77C, 78C, 79C, 80B, 81B, 82B, 83B, 84D, 85C, 86D, 87C, 88A, 89D, 90A

Correct answers and explanations for exam 3:

1. A brand new federal law imposing privacy requirements has been drafted. Which party has the last word when it comes to accepting the law?
A. The house of representatives
B. The president
C. Congress (correct)
D. The supreme court
Explanation:
Congress has the last word. It is not the house of representatives, because it needs both the senate and the house. The president has veto authority, but congress can overrule that veto.

2. A brand new law has been accepted, granting some freedom as regards personal information to organizations. Which party has the last word when it comes to adhering to the law?
A. The Federal Trade Commission
B. The U.S. supreme court (correct)
C. The legislative branch
D. The president
Explanation:
The U.S. supreme court is the highest court in the U.S., and therefore the correct answer.

3. Which of the following laws contains private right of action?
A. The Gramm-Leach-Bliley Act
B. The Health Insurance Portability and Accountability Act
C. The Family Educational Rights and Privacy Act
D. The California Consumer Privacy Act (correct)
Explanation:
Of the options above, only the California Consumer Privacy Act provides private right of action.

4. Circuit courts are appealed to after a lower court. How many circuit courts are there?

A. 94
B. 13 (correct)
C. 50
D. 23

Explanation:
There are 13 circuit courts in the United States.

5. Which of the following is true regarding privacy and the U.S. Constitution?

A. The U.S. Constitution arguably does not provide any privacy protection
B. Privacy is not explicitly mentioned, but the right to be let alone is
C. The U.S. Constitution arguably provides implicit privacy protection (correct)
D. There can never be explicit privacy protection in the U.S. Constitution

Explanation:
The U.S. Constitution provides some privacy protection, such as in the Fourth Amendment which protects against unreasonable searches and seizures by the state. The right to be let alone is also provided in the constitution but in the California Constitution not the U.S. Constitution.

6. The 'code of federal regulations' is administrative law. Which of the following is true regarding administrative law?

A. The Health Insurance Portability and Accountability Act privacy rule is not an example of administrative law
B. Administrative law does not have to go through the legislative process (correct)
C. The Health Insurance Portability and Accountability Act security rule is not an example of administrative law
D. Administrative law is based on case law

Explanation:
Administrative laws are rules written by the departments of the executive branch on how laws passed by congress are enforced. Thus, administrative laws do not go through the legislative process.

7. A court does not always have authority over the parties involved. Which of the following is missing in such a case?
A. Subject matter authority
B. A contract between the parties involved
C. Relevant case law
D. Personal jurisdiction (correct)
Explanation:
This is personal jurisdiction, which is the jurisdiction of the court over a specific person sued or charged with a crime. Personal jurisdiction can, for example, be established by physical presence in a certain geographical area over which the court has jurisdiction.

8. You make use of private right of action a federal law provides. Which of the following is the second court you appeal to?
A. The U.S. supreme court (correct)
B. A district court
C. A circuit court
D. The district attorney
Explanation:
The case goes to a district court, which is not an appeal. Then the case goes to the circuit court, which is the first appeal. Finally, the case can go to the U.S. supreme court, which is the second appeal.

9. Which of the following is least likely true regarding contract law?
A. Contracts are not always legally binding (correct)
B. Only the parties of the contract are legally liable
C. When a contract violates a law, it is not enforceable in court
D. There must be mutual intent to be bound
Explanation:
The correct answer is A, but it is vaguely phrased. A contract is always legally binding if the contract is valid. The contract being valid is implied, but not the only way you can interpret the phrasing. There will be vague phrasing like this on the exam.

10. The General Data Protection Regulation applies to the personal information processing of the European Union's citizens, and under certain conditions even if the personal information is processed in other countries. What can you most applicably call the General Data Protection Regulation also applying in the U.S.?
A. Scope
B. Application
C. Jurisdiction (correct)
D. EU-US Privacy Shield
Explanation:
This would be jurisdiction, which, in a simplified form, is the geographic scope/application, the type of personal information and what is done with it, and by whom.

11. There are several types of liability. How would you describe the difference between criminal and civil liability?
A. Civil liability is about a crime having affected the respondent
B. Criminal liability is about a crime having affected the claimant
C. Civil liability involves mens rea, and criminal liability involves a defendant
D. Civil liability involves a claimant and criminal liability involves the government (correct)
Explanation:
Only the government can bring a criminal case.

12. Which of the following is not part of negligence or invasion of privacy?
A. Mens rea (correct)
B. Duty of care
C. Damages
D. False light
Explanation:
Mens rea involves proving criminal intent. This is relevant in criminal cases, not in tort law.

13. Anonymization is not exactly the same as de-identification. Which of the following best describes the differences?

A. Anonymization requires using pseudonyms, de-identification requires the removal of identifiers

B. Anonymization needs to be done by an external expert, de-identification can be done in-house

C. Anonymization is irreversible, whereas de-identification is not necessarily irreversible (correct)

D. De-identification is stricter than anonymization

Explanation:

De-identification means removing certain elements. However, it does not mean the elements cannot be added back later. Anonymization is per (legal) definition irreversible.

Use this case for the next four questions:
A new indie rock band has released its debut album without being signed by a major record label. This is not by choice, but more because none of the record labels that the band contacted were interested. The independent release of a record means more intense contact with the (yet-to-be-formed) fanbase. Although concerts are generally well attended, the band suspects this to be due to the other bands that perform the same evening, so this deserves some attention.

When the band performs, digital interactive art is incorporated into the music. This involves images being made of the attendees and incorporated into the images projected onto the screen. The band enjoys this process, even though the concertgoers do not seem to pay too much attention to the art. As a memento, the band stores all images and final art on an external hard drive.

The band's music is solely available online. No CDs or vinyl are available with the band's music. This fits the band's philosophy of reducing waste. Although the main music streaming services do not carry the band's music, the band has set up an online purchase system where customers can download a song after purchasing it, or stream it and pay a smaller fee every time the customer listens to the song. The sales data is then analyzed by the band, after which the conclusion is reached that people do not buy the song after streaming it (or even stream it again), hence in order to optimize profits the band disables the option to stream the songs.

14. If the website did not contain a privacy policy or information on the privacy practices, which Fair Information Practice Principle is most likely violated?
A. Collection
B. Data subject access
C. Information quality
D. Disclosure and notice (correct)
Explanation:
Clearly, a privacy notice (when collecting personal information) relates to disclosure and notice. The privacy notice notifies of personal information being collected and discloses how and which/what.

15. The band's website does have a privacy policy. However, you later find out that more personal information was collected than was mentioned in the website's privacy policy. Which of the following is most likely true?
A. The Federal Trade Commission can assess civil penalties
B. The Federal Communications Commission can ask the website to enter into a consent decree
C. The Federal Trade Commission can seek compensation (correct)
D. The scenario is neither deceptive nor unfair
Explanation:
The situation constitutes a deceptive trade practice since you were deceived by the information provided about what will be collected. Compensation for deceptive and unfair trade practices is sought by the Federal Trade Commission. Therefore, option C is correct. Option B can also be correct but is less likely since the point here is the harm to the individual. Keep an eye out for answers that are correct but 'less likely' and try to find the trick to figuring out which of the answers is 'most/more likely'.

16. The band sends out regular emails to inform its mailing list consisting of customers and addresses acquired through a data broker. The emails contain information on new merchandise and discounts. Which of the following is required for those emails according to the Controlling the Assault of Non-Solicited Pornography And Marketing Act?
A. Opt-out (correct)
B. Opt-in
C. Sent at certain times only
D. Use a .com email address
Explanation:
The Controlling the Assault of Non-Solicited Pornography And Marketing Act requires an opt-out to be present in commercial emails like this. The same is required in the European Union under the General Data Protection Regulation and ePrivacy directive.

17. When sending emails to a mailing list some recipients might want to be removed from the mailing list. Which of the following is true regarding the removal from the mailing list?
A. The person opting out can be required to show a form of identification
B. A fee can be charged for processing costs
C. The General Data Protection Regulation applies to mailing lists, which grants the right to be forgotten
D. Opting out can be allowed by phone (correct)
Explanation:
It is fine to allow opting out by phone, but opting out by phone cannot be required according to the Controlling the Assault of Non-Solicited Pornography And Marketing Act. Option C does not address the question.

18. The Golden State Killer was finally caught after many years, through DNA. Which type of privacy was sacrificed to catch him?
A. Territorial privacy
B. Communications privacy
C. Information privacy
D. Bodily privacy (correct)
Explanation:
The Golden State killer was found through a DNA sample, which is bodily privacy.

19. A hardcopy file that includes personal information has been stolen. In which of the following states is that personal information most likely covered under the state's breach notification law?
A. California
B. New Orleans
C. Georgia
D. Hawaii (correct)
Explanation:
Hawaii's breach notification law includes data in any form, which includes written. The other states with a similar scope are Alaska, Iowa, Massachusetts, North Carolina, South Carolina, Washington, and Wisconsin.

20. Websites in the European Union are required to communicate certain information about how they deal with personal information. Of which Fair Information Practice Principle is this an example?
A. Choice and consent
B. Use and retention
C. Data subject access
D. Notice (correct)
Explanation:
This is generally referred to as a privacy notice, which falls under notice.

21. When a large organization fails to inform a person on which other organizations his/her personal information is shared with, which Fair Information Practice Principle is most likely violated?
A. Disclosure and notice (correct)
B. Collection limitation
C. Choice
D. Security safeguards
Explanation:
This also falls under notice. Choice could also be applicable here, but there is not enough information here to conclude whether or not choice is applicable (whether he/she is given a choice).

22. Privacy by Design is a concept embedded in certain laws. Which of the following type of cookies lends itself least to Privacy by Design?
A. Tracking cookies
B. Flash cookies (correct)
C. Functional cookies
D. Analytical cookies
Explanation:
Flash cookies are least likely compliant with the principles of Privacy by Design. This is because they are stored and accessed by Adobe Flash, meaning your browser cannot refuse or delete them.

23. Ever since the General Data Protection Regulation came into force, organizations are giving privacy more attention and many are implementing a privacy program. Which of the following is least likely in charge of the implementation of such a privacy program?
A. The data protection officer (correct)
B. The privacy officer
C. The CEO
D. A designated privacy program manager
Explanation:
A data protection officer needs to be independent and needs to independently assess whether the organization follows the applicable privacy laws. If the data protection officer is in charge of the privacy program, including ownership of the goals and the budget, independence might be lost. Therefore, the data protection officer is not the same as a privacy officer.

24. Data breaches can require prompt action, and even external communication. Who is generally responsible if a data breach response is inadequate?
A. The organization's data protection officer
B. The organization's chief security officer
C. The organization's privacy officer
D. The organization's CEO (correct)
Explanation.
The CEO is ultimately responsible. The data protection officer will never be responsible, unless (perhaps) the data protection officer gave bad advice.

25. Employee training can benefit an organization. Which of the following is least likely true regarding employee training?
A. Employee training reduces security incidents
B. Data breaches are detected faster
C. The privacy of both employees and customers improves
D. Employee training ensures compliance (correct)
Explanation:
Employee training is effective, but it is not a magic bullet. It therefore cannot ensure compliance.

26. Which of the following is least likely true in the case of a data breach involving a data processor?
A. The data processor has to inform the data subjects (correct)
B. An investigation needs to be initiated by the data controller
C. If the data processor breached the contract, it can be held accountable
D. The data protection authority needs to be informed
Explanation:
The data processor works on behalf of (contracted by) the data controller. It thus informs the data controller, and the data controller is responsible for informing the data subjects.

27. Organizations cannot keep personal information forever. Which of the following is not a consideration for determining the retention period of personal information?
A. Whether the personal information has served its purpose
B. Available storage space (correct)
C. The legal requirements
D. The completion of the processes using the personal information
Explanation:
Whether an organization has enough storage is not a legal consideration (no law requires storage space), nor is it a realistic consideration (storage space is not necessarily expensive).

28. Which of the following is most likely false regarding the international use of personal information?
A. When multiple organizations are involved, a contract is needed
B. Data inventories are done for the whole chain
C. Public personal information does not need protection (correct)
D. When transferring personal information to a third party, there needs to be a legal basis to do so
Explanation:
Contrary to what you might expect, there are still laws that require the protection of public personal information when using it (such as the General Data Protection Regulation). This makes sense when you consider that the original public personal information may be deleted, and that when using public personal information you can create new (non-public) personal information (for example the results of an analysis, of a sales record added to the name obtained from a public register).

29. Which of the following is the best strategy for international privacy law compliance?
A. Apply Binding Corporate Rules
B. Comply with the Fair Information Practice Principles (correct)
C. Appoint a privacy officer
D. Ask for consent before collecting personal information
Explanation:
The Fair Information Practice Principles are incorporated into many privacy laws. It is therefore a good strategy to comply with them, as this will likely take care of some requirements of the applicable privacy laws. Binding Corporate Rules is the second-best option, but this will only apply to part of the personal information, and therefore does nothing for laws other than the General Data Protection Regulation.

30. Which of the following is an important privacy by design consideration when developing a global IT system?
A. That the data protection officer has the highest level of access
B. That the chief information security officer has the highest level of access
C. That consent can be withdrawn (correct)
D. That the IT system is properly tested
Explanation:
If the system only allows for permanent records, consent cannot be withdrawn. Regardless of whether any law requiring this, it is a good privacy practice, and privacy by design means including good privacy practices by default.

31. Which of the following is most likely true regarding the retention period of personal information?
A. A purpose of personal information can be changed, and the retention period can be extended without consent
B. The Family Educational Rights and Privacy Act contains a retention period for directory information
C. Personal information is required to be deleted after the retention period is over (correct)
D. The General Data Protection Regulation contains specific retention periods for types of personal information
Explanation:
The period after which something needs to be deleted is the retention period. Option C is therefore correct. The other options are false.

32. You receive personal information from an affiliate in the European Union with a special addition to the contract. Which of the following is false?
A. The contract constitutes a model contract
B. The contract constitutes Binding Corporate Rules (correct)
C. The contract constitutes standard contractual clauses
D. Only the personal information specified in the contract is protected
Explanation:
Model contracts and standard contractual clauses are the same thing, namely a contract, addition to, or changes in a contract, specifying how personal information from the European Union can be used and how it needs to be protected. Binding Corporate Rules does not refer to a contract but refers to a set of rules an international organization can implement in order to be allowed to use personal information from the European Union. Both of these methods are valid under the General Data Protection Regulation.

Use this case for the next three questions:
With the introduction of smartphones, many applications have been developed. Installing these applications requires just a few touches of the screen. This includes many games as well, most of them not age-restricted. One of these games is a colorful video game in which you play a dinosaur collecting bones and rocks. It has become quite popular, and children in schools all over the U.S. are boasting about their high scores.

The game itself is constantly being developed. Most of the development effort goes into adding new looks for the dinosaurs and new levels. Although the game is free to download and play, new additions to the game need to be purchased. These can be purchased within the game, without the need to add a credit card number every time. This is made possible due to blanket permission in the terms and conditions, which most people merely skim or skip.

Parents are furious since they are generally the ones installing the game. In addition, the credit card number is taken from the app store and has not been entered into the game, creating the impression that there is no possibility to charge for anything that is done in the game. The game is designed in a way so that it is difficult to progress without the purchase of at least some upgrades.

Another stream of revenue is generated through analysis of how the players react to triggers in the game and how they interact with certain elements. Insight into this is provided to researchers at a large university, which pays a fee to the video game company.
The game also contains in-game advertisements, where the player is shown an advertisement between levels based on the profile created for that player. There is the option to remove the advertisement, but that option will need to be purchased.

33. The company implements a privacy program to improve the player's privacy. Which of the following is the most likely starting point?
A. A data inventory
B. A data flow map
C. Raising employee awareness and involvement (correct)
D. Hiring a privacy officer
Explanation:
Employee awareness and involvement are important first steps. You cannot start with the other steps before employees are involved. For example, you will need the employees to be aware of what is required and tell you which personal information they use in order to be able to create a data inventory.

34. Privacy programs such as the one implemented by the company generally contain several elements. Which of the following is the least likely part of a privacy program?
A. A data breach response procedure
B. An employee training program
C. Hiring privacy staff
D. A data loss prevention campaign (correct)
Explanation:
Data loss prevention has more to do with security than with privacy. Although you cannot have privacy without security, of the options provided this one is most related to a different discipline, and therefore less likely (but not impossible) to be included in a privacy program.

35. The company found out a data breach occurred and player data was leaked. When is the company going to report it?
A. At the most expedient time, without unreasonable delay (correct)
B. Immediately after discovering a security incident occurred
C. When the investigation into the incident has finished
D. When the company finds out it has a legal responsibility to notify
Explanation:
This is the phrasing close to the terminology used in most privacy laws. Some laws will have a specific deadline, but the addition of a phrase initiating 'as soon as reasonably possible'.

36. Data breaches can require notifying certain parties. Which of the following will least likely need to be notified in case of a data breach?
A. Someone whose encrypted medical data was lost (correct)
B. Someone who was supposed to receive an email, but it was inadvertently sent to the wrong person
C. The state attorney general
D. Someone's personal information crucial to a service was accidentally deleted
Explanation:
Here the point is that the personal information was encrypted. If the level of encryption is sufficient, the data is unreadable and data subjects might not need to be notified. In two-thirds of the states, the state attorney general needs to be informed.

37. Which of the following is the most important consideration when storing personal information on a cloud server?
A. What type of personal information will be stored
B. Where the personal information will be physically stored (correct)
C. The encryption method used
D. Whether you are the data controller or the data processor
Explanation:
The location where personal information is stored can result in different (privacy) laws being applicable. It is therefore important to take location into consideration when deciding.

38. Which of the following is most relevant for role-based access control?
A. Data classification (correct)
B. Storage location
C. Data flow diagram
D. Filetype
Explanation:
All of these options can be relevant, but data classification likely contains the label public/sensitive/confidential, or similar labels useful for role-based access control.

39. What did the Schrems II case result in?
A. An adequacy decision being repealed
B. Canada's private sector being considered adequate
C. Limitations in the use of Binding Corporate Rules
D. EU-US Privacy Shield being declared void (correct)
Explanation:
The cases brought by Max Schrems have resulted in the EU-US privacy shield (and its predecessor Safe Harbor) being declared void.

40. In California there are limitations on the use of social security numbers. Which of the following is least likely forbidden to do with social security numbers?
A. Transmission over Hypertext Transfer Protocol
B. Printing on tax forms/letters (correct)
C. Including the number on an ID card
D. Displaying on a gym membership card
Explanation:
Federal law mandates printing social security numbers on mailings, which includes tax-related mailings.

41. Which of the following is true regarding the Federal Trade Commission's role?
A. The Federal Trade Commission concerns itself with computer security issues (correct)
B. The president has direct control over the Federal Trade Commission
C. Section 6 of the FTC Act is the most important piece of U.S. privacy law
D. The Federal Trade Commission started enforcing privacy issues in the recent years
Explanation:
All are false except for A. Option C might seem correct, but it should be section 5 of the FTC Act which concerns unfair and deceptive trade practices (section 6 is still important, as it gives the authority to perform investigations).

42. To which of the following is the Federal Trade Commission's authority from section 5 of the Federal Trade Commission Act most likely applicable?
A. A bank
B. A transportation company
C. A communications company
D. A retailer (correct)
Explanation:
There are exceptions to the Federal Trade Commission's authority, such as nonprofit organizations. Except for option D, all are exceptions.

43. Which of the following is least likely going to happen if there are several minor problems in an organization's privacy practices brought to the attention of the Federal Trade Commission?
A. The Federal Trade Commission will enter into a consent decree with the company
B. The Federal Trade Commission will launch an investigation into the issues
C. The Federal Trade Commission will work with the company to resolve the problems (correct)
D. The Federal Trade Commission will start an administrative trial
Explanation:
Several minor issues can indicate a pattern, which will result in the Federal Trade Commission at least investigating. If it were just a single minor issue, the Federal Trade Commission would likely not need to investigate and work with the organization to fix the issue.

44. The Federal Trade Commission can seek penalties. Which of the following is true regarding the Federal Trade Commission seeking penalties?
A. The Federal Trade Commission can seek penalties in a district court, up to $43 280
B. The Federal Trade Commission can seek penalties in federal court, up to $43 280 (correct)
C. The Federal Trade Commission can seek penalties in a district court, up to $38 180
D. The Federal Trade Commission can seek penalties in federal court, up to $38 180
Explanation:
The penalties are sought in federal court, and the maximum amount is $43 280.

45. Which of the following does not contain requirements for privacy notices?
A. The Health Insurance Portability and Accountability Act
B. The Gramm-Leach-Bliley Act
C. The Children's Online Privacy Protection Act
D. The Federal Trade Commission Act (correct)
Explanation:
All of these laws require a privacy notice of some sort, except for the Federal Trade Commission Act.

46. What is the Federal Trade Commission's approach under chairman Robert Pitofsky also referred to as?
A. The consent approach
B. The transparency approach
C. The Fair Information Practice Principles approach
D. The notice and choice approach (correct)
Explanation:
Under Robert Pitofsky, the Federal Trade Commission focused on stimulating organizations to provide notice and choice. It is therefore also referred to as the 'notice and choice approach'.

47. IP addresses can, under certain circumstances, be traced back to an individual. In which of the following situations is an IP address most likely considered personal information?
A. In case of a breach of healthcare information (correct)
B. When an unsecured Hypertext Transfer Protocol is used
C. In case a virtual private network is used
D. In case a computer is shared
Explanation:
Option A is vague, but the other options are unlikely to result in personal information. Using HTTP means nothing except how, for example, a website is accessed, using a VPN 'hides' the IP address by changing it and if a computer is shared it is more difficult to determine which data concerns which user.

48. Which of the following statements concerning the Health Insurance Portability and Accountability Act is false?
A. The Health Insurance Portability and Accountability Act is updated by The Health Information Technology for Economic and Clinical Health Act
B. The Health Insurance Portability and Accountability Act is not applicable when payment is in cash
C. The Health Insurance Portability and Accountability Act preempts state law (correct)
D. The Health Insurance Portability and Accountability Act does not prevent medical research
Explanation:
The Health Insurance Portability and Accountability Act does not preempt state law. States are thus free to make stricter laws.

49. Which of the following is the most suitable definition of personal health information falling under the Health Insurance Portability and Accountability Act?
A. Information that can be traced back to a single individual
B. Any individually identifiable health information transmitted or maintained (correct)
C. Any medical information in electronic form, pertaining to a single individual
D. Any information held by covered entities
Explanation:
The important part here is transmitted or maintained.

50. Covered entities are required to provide a privacy notice in most cases. Which of the following would least likely have to provide a privacy notice?
A. A general practitioner
B. A radiologist (correct)
C. A specialist
D. A plastic surgeon
Explanation:
When there is an indirect treatment relationship, a privacy notice does not need to be provided. A radiologist likely has an indirect treatment relationship with the patient.

Use this case for the next three questions:
An online casino has been increasingly successful during a recent pandemic that resulted in many locations having to close for the duration of the pandemic. Its clientele used to consist of those gambling occasionally but has now expanded to those who used to frequent casinos when they were still open.

When a customer signs up on the casino's website, credit needs to be purchased. Depending on the amount of credit purchased, the online casino runs a background check. This takes several forms and is mainly to prevent reputational damage in case of any suspected criminal ties of the customer.

Recently, the casino started providing free kids games. This is intended to introduce children to casino games like poker so that in their later years they have a tie with the casino and will keep gambling. There is no payment required whatsoever, nor are there in-game purchases. The only thing required is an account of the parent or guardian, which the child uses to play teddy bear poker and black Jack the kangaroo.

At some point, the database with users, passwords, and all other user data is stolen and sold on the dark web. This leads to many users being exposed as gamblers, having consequences in both family life and professional life, since employers and spouses are shocked by the gambling behavior of some users.

51. The casino places a cookie that stores the browsing history, but only from the moment of placing the cookie. What is this called?
A. An analytical cookie
B. A third-party cookie
C. A flash cookie
D. A tracking cookie (correct)
Explanation:
Tracking cookies can store the browsing history, and in that way track a user.

52. The casino also uses credit reports. After the casino completes its purposes for the consumer report it collected, it needs to dispose of the consumer report in accordance with the disposal rule. Which of the following is the least suitable method?
A. Pulverizing
B. Compression (correct)
C. Erasing
D. Hiring a document destruction contractor
Explanation:
By compressing something it is made smaller but is not disposed of (it can still be read/used).

53. User preferences are becoming increasingly important, and the casino started to pay attention. Which of the following least likely relates to user preferences?
A. Functional cookies (correct)
B. Analytical cookies
C. Opt-in
D. Opt-out
Explanation:
Functional cookies are required for a website to function, and there is therefore no choice (preference). Analytical cookies can relate to choice since they are not required for the proper functioning of a website, and they can result in the collection of personal information. Opt-in and opt-out clearly indicate a choice, and therefore a user preference.

54. The Genetic Information Nondiscrimination Act contains exceptions in which employers can request genetic information. Which of the following is not one of the exceptions?
A. It is required to comply with an Occupational Safety and Health Act requirement
B. Contaminated DNA needs to be detected
C. The employer purchased it from a public third party
D. The genetic material is not used for discrimination (correct)
Explanation:
Option D is a general statement and not one of the exceptions.

55. There are certain required elements in order for something to be considered a consumer report. Which of the following is not such a requirement?
A. Credit history (correct)
B. Mode of living
C. Character
D. General reputation
Explanation:
Credit history is not necessarily part of a consumer report. However, creditworthiness, credit standing, and credit capacity are.

56. Which of the following is not true regarding the Fair and Accurate Credit Transactions Act and the Fair Credit Reporting Act?
A. The Fair and Accurate Credit Transactions Act amended the Fair Credit Reporting Act
B. The Fair and Accurate Credit Transactions Act added provisions related to identity theft
C. The Fair and Accurate Credit Transactions Act introduced prescreening (correct)
D. The Fair and Accurate Credit Transactions Act was not the first amendment of the Fair Credit Reporting Act
Explanation:
The Fair and Accurate Credit Transactions Act did not introduce prescreening but the Fair Credit Reporting Act did.

57. Which of the following elements are you least likely to find in a consumer report?
A. Character
B. General reputation
C. Mode of living
D. Driving history (correct)
Explanation:
Driving history is not required to be present in a consumer report.

58. Violations of the Fair Credit Reporting Act can lead to having to pay a penalty. What is the maximum penalty for willful violations?
A. $10 063
B. $1 063
C. $5 063
D. $4 063 (correct)
Explanation:
Under the Fair Credit Reporting Act, the maximum penalty for willful violations is $4 063.

59. The Fair and Accurate Credit Transactions Act added a number of consumer protections. Which of the following is not one of those protections?
A. It gave the right to request a free annual consumer report
B. It gave consumers the right the redact the information in their consumer report (correct)
C. Credit card numbers need to be truncated
D. Debit card numbers need to be truncated
Explanation:
Information in a consumer report cannot be redacted by the subject of the consumer report.

60. The Gramm-Leach-Bliley Act Safeguard rule imposed several levels of security. Which of the following is not one of those three levels?
A. Administrative security
B. Technical security
C. Organizational security (correct)
D. Physical security
Explanation:
The three levels are Administrative, Technical, and Physical security. Organizational security is not one of the levels.

61. The Family Educational Rights and Privacy Act is limited to educational institutes which receive federal funding. How is the Family Educational Rights and Privacy Act also known?
A. The Educational Privacy Act
B. The Buckley Amendment (correct)
C. The National School Amendment
D. The Clinton Amendment
Explanation:
The Buckley Amendment is a different name for the Family Educational Rights and Privacy Act. This refers to the supporter of the Family Educational Rights and Privacy Act, senator James Buckley.

62. Which of the following is the best definition of 'education record' under the Family Educational Rights and Privacy Act?
A. Any academic achievement and/or result stored in the school's records, either digital or physical
B. Any academic achievement stored in a record of the education institution, except athletic achievements
C. Any record maintained on a student, including applicant records
D. Any record maintained by the school directly related to a student (correct)
Explanation:
Although option D misses 'on behalf of', it is still the most complete definition of education record.

63. A complaint can be filed if parents or students think their rights have been violated under the Family Educational Rights and Privacy Act. Which of the following investigates the complaint?
A. The Family Policy Compliance Officer (correct)
B. The Federal Trade Commission
C. The Federal Communications Commission
D. The Department of Justice
Explanation:
The Family Policy Compliance Officer is the one investigating such complaints.

64. Which of the following is false regarding the Telemarketing Sales Rule?
A. The Telemarketing Sales Rule was issued by the Federal Trade Commission
B. Requests to call back must be respected
C. Call only between 8 am and 8 pm (correct)
D. Records need to be retained for at least 24 hours
Explanation:
The hours are 8 am – 9 pm, not 8 am – 8 pm. All other options are correct.

65. Which of the following is true regarding caller ID information and the Telemarketing Sales Rule?
A. The telemarketer must submit its own name and phone number
B. Telemarketers are liable when caller ID information does not reach the customer
C. If the calling equipment does not support caller ID, then the telemarketer can provide this information verbally
D. The phone number used to call may be substituted with the customer-service phone number (correct)
Explanation:
Option D is correct. Option A may seem correct, but the phone number may be substituted by that of the seller.

66. When is a seller not allowed to call a person part of the National Do Not Call Registry?
A. When it concerns a prospect
B. When it concerns a customer
C. When the customer bought its product less than two years ago (correct)
D. When the person inquired about the seller's goods two months ago
Explanation:
The maximum period in which a seller can call is within 18 months of a purchase, not two years. Option D is phrased misleadingly because the maximum period is three months, so the two months fall within that period.

67. In which of the following cases is it least likely allowed for law enforcement to perform interceptions?
A. The police expect an email to be sent at a certain time and intercept it
B. The communication is transmitted between two computers only, and not sent over a public network (correct)
C. Somehow the owner of the computer agreed to intercepting his/her computer's transmissions
D. The detective leading the investigation has one serious suspect and wants to see the messages sent to other potential suspects
Explanation:
If the network is public, it is more likely to get an interception authorized. Therefore, if the network is private, it is less likely to get an interception authorized.

Use this case for the next three questions:
An online dating application is focused on the safety of its users. This has resulted in many features, such as video calling before going on a date, indicating that a date is going to happen with a specific person so that the police can be informed in case something happens. Users have to consent to all this access in certain regions since it can be considered quite invasive.

The latest feature of the dating application is only available for a high fee. This feature allows users to run the profile through an internet sweep using facial recognition. Not only will this confirm the name the users provided, but this will also lead to revealing any scandals the user was involved in.

Using the dating application's latest feature has led to the exposure of many fake profiles used to scam lonely people out of money. Many websites with exposed profiles have appeared, and the occasional documentary is made about the biggest fish in the scammer pool.

Some of the persons listed on the scammer websites are not actually scammers. This is due to inaccuracies in the facial recognition software used by the dating application and disgruntled ex-partners falsely listing someone as a scammer.

A lawsuit was started by one of the persons accused of scamming, claiming the dating application falsely exposed them to be scammers. This leads to a lot of publicity, and the dating application does not want to settle since it claims it did not break any laws.

68. The company intends to restrict certain information from certain types of employees. How is this best done?
A. Metadata policy
B. Encryption
C. Specifying access in a policy
D. Role-based access control (correct)
Explanation:
A type of employee can be seen as a role in the context of role-based access control. This question only loosely relates to the case, which is frustrating, but this is what you can encounter on the exam.

69. Which of the following is least likely involved in the process of releasing information during litigation?
A. The CEO (correct)
B. Lawyers
C. IT professionals
D. Privacy professionals
Explanation:
The CEO potentially has a conflict of interest. The other options are all experts on what, from their perspective, can/must be released.

70. The company has made an inventory of which personal information is sent where, all throughout the organization. What is this most likely called?
A. A data inventory
B. A processing agreement
C. A data flow map (correct)
D. Binding corporate rules
Explanation:
Recording where the personal information is sent is recording the flow. The emphasis is on <u>where</u>, meaning it likely describes a data flow map.

71. One party of the lawsuit invokes the Hague convention. What is that party most likely trying to do?
A. Force the other party to comply with international e-discovery
B. Redact a large chunk of data in the discovery procedure
C. Displace the Federal Rules of Civil Procedure (correct)
D. Allow the General Data Protection Regulation to take precedence over U.S. laws
Explanation:
Invoking the Hague convention displaces the Federal Rules of Civil Procedure. This is relevant in case of transborder data.

72. Section 215 of the USA PATRIOT Act has received a lot of attention due to a whistleblower's revelations. Which of the following did that concern?
A. The overruling of the USA FREEDOM Act
B. A large data breach covered up by government officials
C. Targeted collection of call details
D. A database created by the National Security Agency (correct)
Explanation:
After the revelations made by Edward Snowden, the National Security Agency came under fire because of the database with information collected from citizens and noncitizens. You could be tempted by option C, but instead of targeted collection it was substantial and in bulk.

73. Which of the following created a group of independent experts called amicus curiae?
A. The USA PATRIOT Act
B. The Foreign Intelligence Surveillance Act
C. The USA FREEDOM Act (correct)
D. The Federal Trade Commission Act
Explanation:
The expert group with amicus curiae (friends of the court) helps interpret the legality of the U.S. Attorney General's requests.

74. Rule 5.2 of the Federal Rules of Civil Procedure requires attorneys to redact documents before being included in court filings. Which of the following is not such a requirement?
A. The date of birth is redacted to the year of birth
B. For minors, only the initials are included
C. The social security number is redacted to the first four digits (correct)
D. Financial account numbers are reduced to the last four digits
Explanation:
Social security numbers must be redacted to the last four digits, not the first four digits.

75. Workplace privacy in the U.S. is affected by several laws. Which of the following affects the smallest number of people?
A. Tort law
B. The U.S. Constitution (correct)
C. The Consolidated Omnibus Budget Reconciliation Act
D. The Employee Retirement Income Security Act
Explanation:
The U.S. Constitution provides only limited implicit privacy protection and therefore has the smallest impact out of the available options.

76. Workplace privacy is not gained from just one law. Which of the following is the least likely source of workplace privacy in the U.S.?
A. Health and safety laws
B. Security laws (correct)
C. Employee benefit laws
D. Anti-discrimination laws
Explanation:
Although security overlaps with privacy, a security law is unlikely to provide workplace privacy (other than indirectly through an increase in privacy due to fewer security incidents happening).

77. A job applicant declines to authorize a consumer report and is rejected. Which of the following is most likely true?
A. The Fair and Accurate Credit Transactions Act prohibits this
B. The Fair Credit Reporting Act prohibits this
C. Neither the Fair Credit Reporting Act nor the Fair and Accurate Credit Transactions Act prohibits this (correct)
D. Both the Fair and Accurate Credit Transactions Act and the Fair Credit Reporting Act prohibit this
Explanation:
You are free to decline to authorize a consumer report, and the organization is also free to reject your application. No law prohibits this.

78. Criminal background checks are often required. For which of the following is a criminal background check most likely required?
A. For employees from abroad
B. For Health and Safety professionals
C. For persons working with children (correct)
D. Persons working with heavy machinery
Explanation:
Almost every state has a law requiring criminal background checks for people working with children.

79. The Americans with Disabilities Act creates restrictions that influence the hiring process. Which of the following can most likely discriminate against 'a qualified individual with a disability because of the disability of such individual'?
A. A factory, where the manager thinks hiring a disabled person might upset the rest of the workers
B. An office manager, not wanting to make the office wheelchair accessible
C. A shop owner, afraid the disability causes absence disrupting business (correct)
D. A company where being part of the corporate baseball team is an unofficial part of the job
Explanation:
Organizations with fewer than 15 employees are not bound by the Americans with Disabilities Act. A small shop likely has fewer than 15 employees.

80. Lie detector tests are quite invasive. Which of the following is true regarding lie detector tests in the workplace?
A. An employee may refuse to take a lie detector test, but the employer may interpret the refusal as a negative sign
B. An employee can refuse to take a lie detector test and the employer cannot punish the employee (correct)
C. Employment at will allows for an employer to fire an employee who refuses a lie detector test
D. In case taking a lie detector test is required to judge an employee's character rather than investigate an offense, it can be required
Explanation:
The Employee Polygraph Protection Act prohibits adverse action if an employee refuses to take a lie detector test.

81. Which of the following is least likely restricted under the Washington Biometric Privacy law HB 1493?
A. A driver's license
B. An implanted chip (correct)
C. Nose dimensions
D. Freckle pattern
Explanation:
Information on an implanted chip is not biometric data, so option B is the correct answer. Option A is wrong because Washington driver's licenses contain height and weight, which are biometric data.

82. Which of the following is not true under the New Jersey Personal Information and Privacy Protection Act?
A. Retailers may only retain limited information from a customer's ID
B. A retailer can collect specific ID information to detect repeat customers (correct)
C. Information from an ID card can only be collected if it falls under one of the allowed purposes
D. A violation can result in having to pay $2 500
Explanation:
Collecting ID information to detect repeat customers is not permitted use.

83. A company is subject to a rule in a regulation to implement the California Privacy Rights Act. Which of the following most likely created the rule in question?
A. The Federal Trade Commission
B. The California Consumer Privacy Protection Agency (correct)
C. The Federal Communications Commission
D. The state attorney general
Explanation:
The California Consumer Privacy Protection Agency makes rules for the implementation of the California Privacy Rights Act. This is the state-level regulatory agency established by the California Privacy Rights Act.

Use this case for the next two questions:
A museum's newest exhibition includes a large number of interactive digital projects. This results in the art being different at every visit, which attracts visitors from all over the country.

One piece of art involves a camera allowing the visitor to manipulate a digital sculpture in real-time through gestures made in front of the camera. A print-out can then be emailed to the visitor if an email address is provided. Unbeknownst to the visitors, all these images are stored by the creator of the art.

Another piece of art scans the visitor and then manipulates the image to let the visitor see how he or she would have looked in the different periods of time, ranging from the prehistoric ages to the 1990s. This piece of art allows for the option to post the generated images on social media, as long as a specific hashtag is used to link the image to the exhibition.

84. If the museum contracts a third party to perform a task involving the personal information generated in the art exhibition, what is that third party?
A. A data controller
B. A co-controller
C. A data subject
D. A data processor (correct)
Explanation:
The tasks with the personal information are performed at the request of another company (data controller), and therefore is a data processor.

85. The museum has a contract with each of the artists that display their work. A disagreement arises, and the museum goes to court to force the artist to comply with the terms of the contract. A judge decides not to enforce the contract between the company and the artist. Which of the following is most likely the case?
A. The consideration is disproportionate
B. The offer is disproportionate
C. The contract violates a law (correct)
D. The counterparty cannot uphold the contract
Explanation:
If the contract violates a law, it is likely not going to be upheld. This is not restricted to containing consideration, offer, and acceptance.

86. Which of the following is most likely going to result in data destruction compliance?
A. Encrypting personal information irreversibly, after the collection purposes have been fulfilled
B. An organization with a role-based access control policy
C. Implementing physical controls to prevent unauthorized access
D. Deleting personal information from company backups (correct)
Explanation:
Backups are often forgotten, but personal information on backups also needs to be deleted. Option D is therefore correct. Option A may seem correct, but encryption is not irreversible.

87. Which of the following is not a requirement under the California Consumer Privacy Act for it to apply?
A. The organization has an annual gross revenue of $25 million
B. 50% or more of annual revenue due to the sale of personal information
C. The organization is located in California (correct)
D. The organization shares the personal information of 50 000 or more consumers for commercial purposes
Explanation:
The California Consumer Privacy Act can also apply outside of California if a company does business in California.

88. In Massachusetts, which of the following is least likely required when processing a name and sensitive data element under 201CMR17 "Standards for the protection of personal information of residents of the Commonwealth"?
A. Allow data subject access (correct)
B. Appoint a person to be responsible for information security
C. Monitor the effectiveness of security measures
D. Restrict physical access to the personal information
Explanation:
Data subject access is not required.

89. All states have enacted breach notification laws. Which of the following are you least likely to find in these laws?
A. Information on whom to notify
B. The threshold for having to notify
C. Whether to notify the state attorney general
D. The role of the privacy officer (correct)
Explanation:
The role of privacy officer is not included in most (if not all) breach notification laws. In addition, compared to the other options it can be argued to have the smallest impact on properly handling a data breach.

90. Regardless of in which state a data breach takes place, action is likely required. In response to a data breach, which of the following is the least important to consider?
A. The legal basis under which the personal information was collected and stored (correct)
B. Which laws are applicable
C. What is considered to be personal information
D. The location of the cloud server
Explanation:
The legal basis for the collection is important to consider <u>before</u> collecting personal information. The legal basis does not influence the adverse consequences a data subject can suffer, nor the responsibility of the organization to notify.